A Passionate LIFE

LIFESHAPES

A
Passionate

LIFE

MIKE BREEN AND WALT KALLESTAD

Building the New Generation of Believers

COOK COMMUNICATIONS MINISTRIES
Colorado Springs, Colorado • Paris, Ontario
KINGSWAY COMMUNICATIONS LTD
Eastbourne, England

NexGen® is an imprint of
Cook Communications Ministries, Colorado Springs, CO 80918
Cook Communications, Paris, Ontario
Kingsway Communications, Eastbourne, England

A PASSIONATE LIFE
© Copyright 2005 by Mike Breen and Walt Kallestad

First printing 2005
Printed in the United States of America
1 2 3 4 5 6 7 8 9 10 Printing/Year 10 09 08 07 06 05

Cover Design: Bill Chiaravalle, BrandNavigation, LLC
Cover Photo: PhotoDisc

Mike Breen is the creator and developer of the LifeShapes material (formerly called LifeSkills) and the eight (8) shapes as a memorable method of discipleship.

ISBN: 0-78144-269-9

This book is dedicated to Harry and Beckie Butler. Without their friendship and support, so much would never have happened.

—Mike

This book is dedicated to my first grandbaby, Sevannah Joy Cole and all future generations that they might experience the passionate life with Jesus Christ.

—Walt

ACKNOWLEDGMENTS

*L*ifeShapes is not so much a teaching as it is a testimony in "A Passionate Life." I acknowledge this by mentioning some of the stars of the story, people like Walt Kallestad, Paddy Mallon, and Paul Maconochie. In this acknowledgment I would like recognize the role of the less visible ones. First Bob and Mary Hopkins (only partially recognized previously) who have served tirelessly and helped forward the mission of LifeShapes down through the years. They helped especially in the formulation of the Triangle and in the development of the strategy of evangelism found in the Octagon. I would like to acknowledge Ken Blanchard, whose initial teachings on the four phases of leadership were partially responsible for the development of the Square. Others like John and Liz Lovell, Andrew and Margaret Wooding-Jones, Tim and Alisa Phenna should also be recognized for their contribution to this testimony. Still others among the "little people" have had a profound influence on me and my family—the members of the congregations we have served, represented by the Willeys, Val, the Moodys, the Stones, and the Williams'. All these people are part of the story and the Lord knows their role and I'm sure will reward their service. Finally to Susan and Joannah, I would like to give enormous thanks for their help in the preparation of the manuscript for *A Passionate Life*.

—Mike Breen

ACKNOWLEDGMENTS

A big, big thanks to the Cook Communications team (a team of champions). Thanks to Mike Breen and his incredible team. Thanks to all my family, friends, and partners who are living out the passionate life with me. I love you all.

—Walt Kallestad

CONTENTS

MEET THE AUTHORS

*P*astor Walt Kallestad had spent more than twenty years building Community Church of Joy in Phoenix, Arizona, into a seeker-friendly assembly of 12,000 when his heart nearly failed him. In January 2002 Walt suffered a major heart attack; only six-way bypass surgery and the grace of God kept him from going home to heaven at a relatively young age.

The physical trauma forced Walt to take a year-long sabbatical. During this time he did some serious evaluation of the state of his church and the direction in which it was moving—and whether he should continue leading it. He sought counsel from pastors across the country. Finally, a trusted friend gently forced Walt to acknowledge that his huge flock had lost its community, its authenticity—its passion. Besides, who would want to take on the mammoth responsibilities of running a megachurch when he could walk on the cutting edge of modern ministry? And where did that leave Community Church of Joy? Walt's search moved in a new direction: overseas.

Pastor Mike Breen, Rector and team leader of St. Thomas Church (an Anglican and Baptist Church) in Sheffield, England, had grown one of the largest churches in England with more than two thousand attending weekly worship, 70 percent of which are under the age of 35.

One of Walt's peers suggested he visit St. Thomas Church in Sheffield, England. One visit to St. Thomas left Walt amazed at the depth of spiritual growth and authentic community he sensed among the people. One conversation with Mike Breen left him intrigued with a new concept and approach to teaching and discipleship: LifeShapes.

Mike had spent the better part of a decade developing this visually oriented teaching tool. LifeShapes had certainly proved its effectiveness among the members of this largely twenty- and thirty-something congregation. It was helping them not only to understand biblical principles on a deeper level, but also to apply those principles to their lives. St. Thomas Church had become a church passionate to know Christ and to make him known.

Mike and Walt made a connection in that conversation. It proved to be a life-changing moment . . . a *kairos* moment. God stepped into the circumstances of these two men and pulled the loose ends of their worlds together. Creator of LifeShapes, Mike, his wife, Sally, and their three children had recently moved to the U.S. to teach at Fuller Theological Seminary in Pasadena, California, serve on the staff of Walt's church in Glendale, Arizona, and travel the country speaking on LifeShapes. Now, as a staff member of Community Church of Joy, Mike is teaching the principles of LifeShapes and helping the church to once again reflect the foundation of its name: community.

INTRODUCTION

*A*h-h-h! The hot tub. What could be better? At that moment, the Breen family's health club membership fee seemed well worth it. My wife, Sally, and our three children—Rebecca, Elizabeth, and Sam—enjoyed all the typical instruments of torture, like weights and treadmills. But the hot tub was the place for me while we lived in Sheffield, England.

I was relaxing in the hot tub one week when my daughters came up to me and asked if I had tried the Sun Shower yet.

"I don't even know what a Sun Shower is," I admitted. "What is it?" Did I even want to know?

They pointed. "It's that white tube over by the pool. You stand up in it and get a tan, but you also get totally refreshed. It's like standing on the beach in South Carolina."

Now, as far as the Breen family is concerned, the beaches of South Carolina are the closest things to perfection that you can find here on earth. With my daughters' exuberant assurance that I couldn't possibly regret it, I agreed to give it a try.

"What does it take?" I asked.

"A pound for three minutes."

So I rummaged for a one-pound coin and walked over to the Sun Shower. The door opened to a room the size of a small closet. Nothing looked too dangerous, so I stepped in and closed the door. Still not certain of what I was doing, I made sure to read the instructions posted on the wall clear through. Following them carefully, I put on a pair of goggles hanging in there and shut my eyes tightly. Nothing happened.

Of course. The one-pound coin.

I opened my eyes, took off the goggles, put the coin in the slot, pulled the goggles back on, and waited. Nothing. Well, I heard a slight whirring sound and a few clicks, but I felt nothing. This in no way resembled the beach in South Carolina.

When the three minutes were up, the whirring stopped and I stepped out.

"What did you think?" my daughters asked.

They looked so excited. Clearly they thought the Sun Shower was a fantastic idea. How could I possibly let them down? But I had to be honest.

"Well," I said, "I guess I just don't get it. I mean, it was okay, but probably something you girls would like better."

Elizabeth and Rebecca were profoundly disappointed. They had wanted so badly for me to share their experience, and I hadn't. Frankly, I thought the whole thing was rather strange, but I didn't say much about it.

The next week we were back at the health club. Rebecca and Elizabeth came up to me with renewed fervor.

"Dad," they said, "this time try it for six minutes. Maybe three minutes wasn't enough for you to start feeling the effects. Give it six minutes, okay?"

I started to tell them how silly the whole thing was, but they were giving me those looks. You know the ones. No father could say "No."

So back I went to the white tube. I stepped inside the room, pulled the door closed, read the instructions, put on the goggles and squeezed my eyes shut. Nothing.

Oh, right. The coins. Goggles off, coins in, goggles on. I closed my eyes again and waited. Six minutes is a long time to wait when you're standing in an enclosed booth with your eyes shut, listening to whirring and clicking noises. When it was over, I took off the goggles and hung them back on the hook and left.

Elizabeth and Rebecca were anxiously waiting for me. "How was it this time, Dad? Did you feel the effects this time?"

I looked at my daughters' expectant faces. "I don't really think it's for me."

They thought I was completely daft.

"This is something for you and your friends to enjoy," I said. "Maybe I'm just too old to get the full benefits of it."

One thing I must say for my children: they don't give up easily. The next week they were ready.

"Dad, try it this time for nine minutes. You'll really love it if you give it enough time. Nine minutes should do it for you. C'mon, Dad!"

I looked over at Sally for support, but she just gave me the "You got yourself into this, get yourself out" look. So off I went for the third time to the Sun Shower. I went in the tube, pulled the door shut, and read the instructions clear through for the third time. They hadn't changed a word. I put on the goggles and closed my eyes.

Sigh. The coins.

Goggles off, coins in, goggles on, eyes closed. Let me tell you, if six minutes is a long time, then nine minutes is a very long time to stand in a closet in the dark listening to clicks and whirrs. So I took a chance and opened my eyes—only to find that I could see right through the goggles. Looking around, I wondered if I would get more of a tan if I stood closer to the mirror.

Then I saw some things that looked like coat hooks on the wall. M-m-m. I thought that maybe they were there to reflect the rays. Standing still for nine minutes was not much more interesting than keeping my eyes closed for nine minutes, so I turned around.

I saw a doorknob. What was this? I turned the knob, and the door opened to a room filled with the most refreshing light rays and replicated ocean breeze I could ever imagine.

For three weeks I had been standing in the changing room.

All this time I thought I was having the experience I was supposed to have. I had tried to work up feelings of refreshment, but I knew that they weren't real. As hard as I tried, I just didn't get it! Finally I had experienced the real thing.

Is your experience with Jesus like this? Have you been standing in the changing room for weeks and months, even years, wondering what's so great about being a Christian? You see others at church or in your small group, and they talk about how wonderful it is to know Jesus—really know him like you know your best friend—and you long for that same experience. Maybe you even try to put on a good show, telling your friends how much Jesus means to you even though it's not true. Perhaps you attend church every week but come away feeling empty, thinking it's a great waste of time. Yet others come out refreshed, so you keep going back, keep putting your money in the coin slot and keep telling your friends what an exhilarating feeling you have too. But you know it isn't working for you.

Jesus would not have invited us to be his friends if he didn't mean it. He would not have called us to follow him if we were not meant to see where he is going. This is what we're inviting you to do: walk with Jesus. It sounds simple, doesn't it? It is simple, but it's not easy. We can help you develop a deeper understanding of what it means to walk with Jesus—to be his follower, his disciple—in a way that you can remember and apply to every situation and relationship in your life.

So what are you waiting for? Come on—open the door. Leave the closet of spiritual emptiness and step into the light of a passionate life!

IS THAT ALL THERE IS?

We work all day, we feed the kids, we clean the bathroom, we go to church; we work all day again, we feed the kids again, we go to choir practice, we catch the news; we go to the store, we do the laundry, and we feed the kids again. You get the picture. Before we know it, years have gone by and we wonder what has become of our lives.

Have we done what we thought we would do by this time?

Have we become who we thought we would become by this time?

Have we sat at the feet of Jesus as much as we wanted to?

It's not difficult to let responsibilities and roles shape our lives. You're a mom or a dad. You're a teacher or a carpenter or a stockbroker. You're a single parent. You're caring for an aging parent. You're working two jobs to pay off medical bills. You're on three ministry teams at church and now have been asked to join the board as well.

And you're human, so you get tired of all this! Soon even things that you care about deeply wear you out and you want a break.

The world is full of the walking weary. Yet that is not the life that Jesus

> The world is full of the walking weary. Yet that is not the life that Jesus called us to live.

called us to live. In Matthew 11:28-29, Jesus says "Come to me, all you who are weary . . . Take my yoke . . . and learn from me. . . ."

Jesus wants to show us a better way to live. When we follow where he leads, amazing things happen. How much richer and satisfying our lives are when we let Jesus shape them.

BEING, NOT DOING

In any city in America we can choose from dozens, if not hundreds, of churches that preach the message of Jesus and his kingdom. In those churches we can join small groups, cell groups, life groups, and home groups. Even without leaving our homes, we can watch Christian television programs or listen to preachers on the radio exhorting and encouraging us. We do our chores or exercise to worship music on our chewing gum-sized MP3 players.

And then there are books. Thousands of them. Every year thousands of newly published Christian books join the tens of thousands already on the shelves. These books tell us how to be a Christian student, a Christian teacher, a Christian parent, a Christian journalist, a Christian spouse. Books tell us how to pray, how to sing, how to think, how to speak as Christians. Some books even claim to tell us what God wants us to drive.

Enough already.

This is not one of those books.

This is not a book about *doing* discipleship.

This is a book about *being* disciples. This is a book that helps us see Jesus. This is a book that helps us see where Jesus is going. This is a book that helps us follow Jesus where he leads us.

JESUS THE RADICAL

Jesus was a radical. He did not fit into the prefabricated mold of Messiah that the Jewish culture had prepared. He did not offer his backing to the established religious community. He showed no interest in influencing the politics of the day. Jesus was a radical from the time he was 12 and dared to go about his Father's business by questioning and instructing the rabbis in the temple (Luke 2:46-49).

In his revolutionary style, Jesus spoke of a kingdom where God ruled as king. Jesus broke into history at a real point in time, died on a real cross, and left behind a real empty tomb. This was no last-ditch effort on God's part to save the world from its woes. This was his plan for bringing his kingdom to earth. The cross and resurrection changed history; now we are pointed toward heaven.

Now here is the amazing part: we can live in this kingdom right now! The kingdom of God is not some far-off, distant, future realm. It is not a state of mind. It is not something we dream about or long for. We are in it! God's kingdom is a real place where we can walk and work and have relationships.

Here is yet another amazing thing about Jesus' announcement of this kingdom. The King wants to live with us!

God is not an absent ruler sending messages through his servants because he can't be bothered to come himself. The Ruler of the kingdom has come to us. He lives in our neighborhood. He invites us to walk with him, to work alongside him, to sit at the supper table with him. And, if we accept his invitation, he says we can live with him forever in his kingdom—starting today.

Living in the kingdom with the king as our guide—that is discipleship. That is what it means to be a follower of Jesus. We have no higher calling.

God is not an absent ruler sending messages through his servants because he can't be bothered to come himself.

The essence of being a disciple is spending time with the Master himself. Walking and working and eating with Jesus is not about rules and regulations. It's not about how many times a month you go to church, or how many verses you read in your Bible every day, or how much of your income you give to the church. God wants us to do all those things, just for different reasons than the Pharisees had. He wants our hearts.

WHICH WAY WILL YOU GO?

Following Jesus is not a part-time occupation. It requires total commitment. It requires fighting against the tide of what's popular. Jesus will not be cheated—he wants everything you have.

In the aftermath of the tsunami that devastated Asia in December 2004, incredible stories of survival have emerged. Many people recount being so quickly submersed in water churning with debris that they didn't know if their struggling was taking them up towards the surface or only farther down into the depths. The survivors were those who were able to find their way up.

When you're struggling against the tide, it's important to know which way is up. We're living in a time of seismic changes in our culture—changes that have left us disoriented in our spiritual journey even as we fight against the tide. But Jesus knows the way. Jesus is our unfailing compass.

We invite you to walk with us in a passionate, intimate life as a follower of Jesus in the kingdom of God. We will show you how to do this in a practical, daily way. No magical formulas or ten-step programs are involved. As a matter of fact, you can find everything we're going to share with you in your own Bible. We are going to look at what Jesus did in teaching his followers two thousand years ago, then suggest ways to do the same things today.

CHAPTER 2

A PASSIONATE PURSUIT

*S*omeone says, "Salt." You think, "Pepper." Someone says "Hot." You think, "Cold." Some associations between words and concepts are automatic. We can't help what we think. On the other hand, some associations are learned, and while they may seem automatic and subconscious, we *can* change them.

Try this one. What one word comes to your mind when you read this list?

- go to church
- study the Bible
- pray
- give money to church
- avoid worldly pleasure

Did you think "Christian"? Not so exciting. If that's what being a Christian is about, then a lot of other options will seem more appealing.

Maybe you would use these phrases if someone asked you to describe "disciple." If so, you're right in there with a lot of people who consider themselves religious—including the Pharisees of Jesus' day who were so irritated by Jesus and his teachings.

The Pharisees knew their religion. They knew what they believed. They knew what they should do and what they should not do. The word *Pharisee* means "separated ones," so that's what they did. They separated themselves from any ungodly influence. These religious leaders were so concerned about keeping God's law that they made up a whole slew of extra laws and practices that would make sure they kept God's law.

Being a Pharisee was a lot of work. But that's not what Jesus had in mind for his followers.

Jesus invited people to follow him. He did not insist on ceremonial hand washing before people sat down to eat. He did not mind if his followers walked through a wheat field on the Sabbath and broke off heads of grain to eat. He was not hung up on religious practices. And he was always hanging around with—even eating with—the worst sort of people. How could this be a path to God? The Pharisees were enraged with indignation and jealousy.

SUPER CHRISTIANS?

Many of us think that the word "disciple" means "super Christian" (someone who is more dedicated to spiritual things than the average Christian) and discipleship is training for the new or nearly new believers so they can look like, talk like, and act like the rest of us. Clear your head of that notion. That's exactly what the Pharisees were doing in Jesus' time! In the midst of the shifting spiritual landscape of today's culture, no one wants to be a "super Christian," no one even wants to *know* a "super Christian."

Too many of us have grown up in broken homes.

Too many of us have been disoriented by tragedy in our lives.

Too many of us have lost faith in cultural institutions, including the church.

Too many of us grow up wondering if anyone really cares about us.

There is no such thing as a "super Christian." They are as fake as the Pharisees, yet we have all been hurt by people wearing that label. What we are longing for is to enter into relationships with people who are not just shiny and pretty on the outside, but who are real and authentic with the life that God has given them, as messy as it may be.

Until the 1990s, family shows dominated television programming. "Family Ties" and "The Cosby Show," while not as traditional as "Leave It to Beaver" or "Father Knows Best," still had Mom and Dad working together to provide a safe harbor for their children.

Since the early 90s, those shows have been replaced with others that reflect real life. "Friends" was the number one show of the 1990s. "Seinfeld" depicted a group of very different people held together not by blood, but by loyalty. Changes in our culture have changed how we define community—yet, community is still what we are all hungry to find. If we no longer have a traditional family to which we can "belong," where can we belong?

> The mega-marketing machine of our culture spends billions to tell us what we can be—if only we will buy their products.

The mega-marketing machine of our culture spends billions to tell us what we can be—if only we will buy their products. Young people find their identities in song lyrics and movie dialogue, on MTV, in brand-name shoes and jeans, in cell phones and wireless Internet. When they get a little older, they look for a house worthy of the image they wish to project and a steadily growing 401(k) fund with just the right mix of mutual funds.

With everyone else in the world telling us who we are, is it any wonder we're confused about who we want to be and how we need others to connect with us?

DON'T TELL ME, SHOW ME

When Jesus walked the roads of Galilee, he used words to teach his students—parables, sermons, prayers. The first disciples passed these on to the next generation of disciples, and to the next. When the gospel writers finally recorded Jesus' words and life several decades after he died, large gatherings of followers listened to the words as they were repeated publicly. The Apostle Paul and other New Testament writers shared their hearts and insights in letters—words—that were passed around from church to church. People learned the Scriptures by hearing and memorizing.

Since the advent of the printing press—and more recently, the Internet—we no longer have to remember something we hear. We can just go look it up again when we need the information. Our advances in technology have come at the cost of our ability to store and retrieve large quantities of information using only our minds. But when information is attached to symbols and shapes, we multiply our ability to remember principles and concepts.

We're living in an increasingly visual society. Small children recognize marketing logos long before they can decode the letters that make up the names of their favorite places. They know a McDonald's when they see the golden arches. They know the red circle with the red dot in the center means Target is nearby. Teenagers wear their clothes and hair just so—much to the consternation of their parents—because they are trying to achieve "the look." Magazines for all ages have a visual edge because information alone is not enough to keep the readers' attention. Some great books have been made into movies (some of the movies not so great), and many adults would quickly agree they'd rather see the movie than read the book. Family games during long car trips have been replaced by DVD players that flip down from the ceiling or the back of the front seat.

When you look at this shape, what do you see?

Right—Mickey Mouse. Now what thoughts does that bring to your mind? A recent vacation to Disneyland or Disney World? A favorite Disney movie? Maybe you thought of some of the characters Walt Disney introduced us to like Goofy, Donald Duck, or Pluto. Or perhaps the more modern Little Mermaid, Nemo, or Buzz and Woody came to mind.

Isn't it amazing how much you can remember and talk about just from seeing two small circles intersect a larger one?

WHY LIFESHAPES?

LifeShapes takes advantage of our tendency to remember what we see longer than we remember what we hear. These eight aspects of kingdom life are easy enough to show using simple shapes, yet deep enough that we will never reach the end of learning even one of them.

I grew up in a Christian home and played an active role in my church. But when I left for college in another part of the country, the pressures to fit in took their toll on my life. I rarely went to church or any Christian groups and soon lost sight of the values I once lived by. It wasn't long before my lifestyle was a world away from the life I once knew.

My *kairos* moment came when I became very ill. As I laid in bed, thinking about how I was supposed to change the direction of my life, I knew that I was going to need somebody to talk to. And so began a long discussion with my friend and mentor Rachel. As we talked, we made a plan for the future. I knew I wanted to straighten my life out but I also knew it would be costly. Many lifestyle changes needed to be made and Rachel was going to help me through those changes. I recognized that a lack of accountability had been a point of weakness for me. Now, with accountability in place, I was feeling like I could take some real steps toward change. It wasn't long before I was well again. Yet the process of the Circle would continue. My *kairos* event led to a renewed relationship with God and it was through accountability and relationship that I could see how I ended up where I was and plan effectively for the future.

—CHLOE

LifeShapes is not a way to teach and apply thousands of biblical principles, or even dozens. Rather, we focus on a few key concepts that will make you a lifelong learner. LifeShapes is a tool that will enable you to cut through the muck of this changing spiritual landscape and get back to Jesus so that you can follow him through these times of seismic change. That means that you will move beyond mere information and learn from Jesus, engage him at a fresh level, and know what he really meant when he first trained his disciples. When you have this framework of truth, you can build biblical principles into your life and grow together with other disciples into an authentic community.

LEARNING FROM THE MASTER

Jesus did not mean his principles for kingdom life to be theoretical. He meant for us to actually live by them! The eight shapes of LifeShapes help us connect the dots between Jesus' kingdom principles and living our every-day lives in ways that honor him. These shapes paint a clear picture through which we can better understand what God intends to do in our personal lives, in the church and in the world. These concepts can shape our lives if we want them to.

- Choosing to Learn from Life
- Living in Rhythm with Life
- Balancing the Relationships of Life
- Defining the Priorities of Life
- Knowing Your Role in Life
- Praying as a Way of Life
- Practicing the Principles of a Vital Life
- Living a Life with a Mission

With these principles, you can leave the world of the walking weary and live a life full of purpose and passion—and teach others to do the same.

This kind of discipleship will raise eyebrows. Jesus was not afraid of scandal. He was not so much concerned with perceptions of public moral-ity as he was with hearts genuinely turned toward God. When we walk in his footsteps, powerful emotions erupt—intense feelings, convictions about authentic discipleship. Life-shaping experiences. A passionate life.

CHAPTER 3

DECISION TIME

Do you ever feel as if the events of your life are beyond your control? That life is happening *to* you as you stand passively by? Life is a challenge. Every day we are each presented with 1,440 new moments in time. What happens in many of those moments *may be* beyond our control, though not beyond *his* control. Yet it is these very moments that make up the sum of our lives—and determine whether we feel like we are living a life of significance or irrelevance.

As a follower and friend of Jesus, you want your life to count—to have a purpose and meaning beyond what is offered to you (sometimes quite attractively) by the world—because you know that it is the kingdom life that will have lasting value. Jesus, our teacher and friend, reveals to us how we can learn from the moments of our lives.

"The time has come," [Jesus] said. "The kingdom of God is near. Repent and believe the good news!"

—Mark 1:14-15

At the very beginning of his earthly ministry, Jesus tells of a great opportunity: God's kingdom is within our reach. To enter the kingdom, however,

The Circle represents our journey into the kingdom of God.

we must go through a process of repentance and belief. The process can be difficult and challenging. Sometimes it is painful. But through this process we learn how to lay down our lives, pick up the cross, and follow Jesus into the kingdom. The Circle represents our journey into the kingdom of God, and time, the *kairos* moments in our lives, is the portal through which we can enter into kingdom living.

WHAT IS A *KAIROS* MOMENT?

In the language of Jesus' day, there are two primary words for "time": *chronos* and *kairos*. The first refers to chronological time, such as when you check the clock to see how long you have to wait for lunch or when you announce that "Dinner will be at eight o'clock."

Kairos, on the other hand, reveals an event that happened at a particular point in time. If that eight o'clock dinner turns out to be the most fun you've had in a long time and you feel some relief from the pressures of your life, then it becomes a *kairos* moment. *Kairos* refers to a significant event—good or bad—that alters your life. Something happened or something was said that made an impact. It may even have made *chronos* time seem to stand still.

Do you remember the day you were married? How about the birth of your first child? Think about a favorite vacation you took with your family. These are all *kairos* moments you cherish. Some *kairos* events, however, leave an impact because of their tragic consequence: the death of a loved one, a divorce, an argument with a coworker, the horrific events of September 11, 2001.

Kairos events may be positive or negative; but they are never neutral. By their very nature, *kairos* moments make an impression on you. Maybe you receive a promotion and a raise at work. The additional money will allow you to move into the size house your family really needs. The new position lets you use your talents in a more creative way. You are more energized than you have been in years.

On the other hand, perhaps you offer a word of encouragement to someone, but the person takes it the wrong way. Others find out and think that you are spreading gossip. You notice the whispers and fingers pointed back at you. You feel anxiety and fear. You are passing through a *kairos* moment. Emotions are a great indicator of *kairos* events. Often the events that trigger negative emotions present the greatest opportunities for growth.

SEIZING OUR TEACHABLE MOMENTS

We humans are an analytical lot. When a *kairos* moment occurs, especially one that stirs up negative emotions, we want to study all the events that led to this crisis with the hope of preventing a similar thing from happening again. We think what we need to learn from our mistakes is how not to ever make that mistake again!

We're looking through the wrong end of the telescope. Instead of looking back at the event to prevent circumstances from converging in the same way again, we need to look forward to the growth that we can experience from it. Rather than focusing on what we want to leave behind from an experience, we should be proactive about what we want forward from the experience as we move into the next task or relationship or season of our lives.

We tend to think of the faith journey as linear, with a starting point (salvation) and an ending point (heaven.) We're headed toward a specific destination, and the road that will get us there is straight and flat. All we have to do is stay on the straight and narrow.

Salvation •••••••••••••••••••••••••••••••➤ **Heaven**

That does not give the best picture of the walk of a disciple. Let us suggest another picture.

THE CIRCLE AS A LIFESTYLE FOR LEARNING

Here you are, walking on what you consider to be a straight path; no unexpected bends in the road, no intersections where you have to make a decision you're not prepared for. Perhaps you have a specific purpose in mind, or perhaps you are simply walking in the general direction that seems best. Then, seemingly out of the blue, a *kairos* moment happens and brings you to a screeching halt.

Now you are at an intersection that requires a reaction, a decision.

You can keep on walking forward, ignoring the door for growth, act as if the event never happened and had no effect on you.

You can stop and refuse to move in any direction at all. The event affects you so strongly that you're not sure you even want to be on this road any longer.

You can go backward to a part of the path you already know and stay where it's familiar and safe.

Or you can pass through the portal and enter into the process of learning—the Circle. What propels us into this process is a *kairos* event. "The *time* has come." It can be positive (getting a promotion) or negative (getting laid off). It can be big (your wedding) or small (a date night with your spouse). But when a *kairos* moment occurs, we must decide whether to enter the Circle. From the moment we step into the Circle, we are in a learning mode. Things will not go back to the way they were before the *kairos* event.

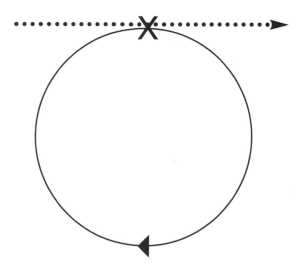

The LifeShapes Circle expands three elements—observe, reflect, and act—of a well-known learning circle into six elements, creating a process that uniquely fits the principles taught by Jesus. Half of the circle concentrates on Repent, with the steps of Observe, Reflect, and Discuss. The other half of the circle brings us around to Believe, with the steps of Plan,

Account, and Act. The additional steps—Reflect, Discuss and Account—provide for the biblical principle of body life. God has called us to be in community with each other and the process of discipleship is best experienced in the context of a faith community.

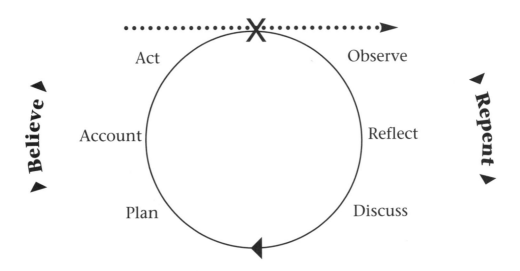

While *kairos* is an event word—something that has a beginning and an end—Repent (*metanoia*) is a process word. So is Believe (*pistis*). The Circle is a process, a lifestyle that does not have a specific beginning and ending. One does not become a disciple of Jesus and stand still; discipleship is a lifestyle of learning. This learning means continually repenting of the way we approach life. It means a change of heart. Having experienced a *kairos* event in our lives, we then begin the process of repentance. But real learning doesn't occur until we move through the belief process—initiating a plan for which we are accountable and that changes our actions.

Most of us have regarded depression as a negative, shameful experience using terms such as "breakdown," when it is important to regard it as a possible signpost towards change. As a Christian counselor, I have been using the context of the learning circle in my practice. I have seen transformation in individuals who have chosen to view depression as a learning event, a signpost from God. It may be discipline, it may be guidance but it is something we need to responsibly process and respond to.[*]

—*Dr. Angus Bell*

Why Change?

Doesn't everyone long for a passionate life? We love passionate and enthusiastic people; they carry something of the nature of God with them. In fact the word enthusiasm derives from a Greek word *enthousiasmos*, that comes from *entheos*, "having the god within." It's as though the human heart was created for passion and enthusiasm, yet as we face life's challenges we can suffer a sequence of losses and disappointments that kill our passion. Missed opportunities, broken relationships, the stresses and strains of life that cause us hurt take their toll.

Eventually we try to protect ourselves and our passion is gradually restrained, starved, and weakened. We begin to feel less alive as a result. This is a dangerous position to be in because a hungry heart is a persistent predator looking to devour anything that will give temporary respite to the ache within. Our hearts become more vulnerable to the quick fix and can be drawn into a season of darkness and depression. We don't have to go there— and if we find ourselves there, we don't have to stay there.

---

* For up to date information on other products related to using the Learning Circle in the context of counseling, visit www.lifeshapes.com

Jesus loves you too much to leave you as you are. As his disciple, you are called to a life of constant renewal, revival—of change. By learning how to identify the *kairos* moments in your life and choosing to enter into the process of repentance and belief, you can transform the way you view the challenges of your life. You can find hope and healing for your past, present, and future. You can face life enthusiastically.

CHAPTER 4

CHANGE IS GOOD?

*A*s followers of Jesus, we are called continually to change how we think. The Christian's life has an ongoing aspect of change. Walking as a disciple of Jesus means constantly growing and changing inwardly as you take on more of the character of the Teacher. Every day—multiple times—we have the opportunity to say, "I'm not going to be like that any more. I'm not going to snap back at the coworker who was rude to me. I'm not going to yell at my kids about leaving their bikes in the driveway again. I'm not going to ignore how hard my spouse is working so I can do what I want to do." Repentance is not about judgment. It's about change.

Repentance is essential if we are to grow as disciples, but it is not always easy. In fact, most of the time it is not easy. Facing our failings is something we want to put off, like a trip to the dentist or bathing the cat. But hiding or ignoring our failings does not make them go away, and we will not progress in our walk with Jesus unless we go through the Repent side of the Circle.

REPENTANCE IS ESSENTIAL

In Mark 1:15, Jesus' first command to us, the first part of the Circle, is to Repent. Often we encounter strong resistance when we bring up this word, because it stirs up images of heavy-handed preachers handing out condemnation rather than grace. But repentance is more than just how we feel or how we react after we have done something wrong. The word "repent" comes from the Greek word *metanoia*, which means to change one's mind. Change is a vital part of the life of a follower of Jesus. Once we change on the inside, the new attitude will affect our outward actions.

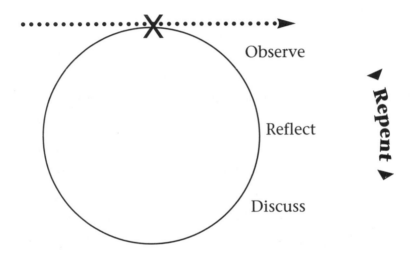

Observe

As we ponder the Repent half of the Circle, let's follow a story in Jesus' life and teaching from Matthew 6. The first step in repentance is to Observe.

Jesus and his followers were wrapping up a long day. He had gone up on a hillside and taught what we commonly call the Sermon on the Mount. In this day-long teaching, Jesus outlined the radical lifestyle that he calls his followers to adopt. He talked about real-life issues like murder, adultery, divorce, lying, revenge, loving your enemy, giving to the needy, prayer and fasting, and the love of money. Except for the prayer and fasting, it sounds like a prime-time soap opera. Everybody has a secret that no one else is supposed to know about. But Jesus knows. He talks about these subjects in a way that forces them to the forefront.

We can easily imagine how this led to the internal pressure that becomes a *kairos* event. Listeners start thinking about the things they're hiding. What if everything falls apart? When this happens, anxiety and worry set in. So Jesus addressed this real-life reaction we humans are prone to.

Do not worry about your life, what you will eat or drink or about your body, what you will wear. Is not life more important than food, the body more important than clothes?

—Matthew 6:25

Jesus knows what is happening in his followers' hearts, so he takes them through the process that will set them free. He begins with observation. He tells them to look at the birds. Okay, birds. The disciples had the Pharisees breathing down their necks, and Jesus is looking at the birds. We can hear them asking, "What does that have to do with what I'm worried about?" It's probably a good thing Matthew doesn't tell us exactly what the disciples said in this situation. It's to their benefit that most of what they talked about with Jesus is not recorded. A lot of what we do know they said was a little slow on the draw. But Jesus is a patient teacher.

> The disciples had the Pharisees breathing down their necks, and Jesus is looking at the birds.

Jesus is getting his followers to observe their own lives by having them look at something else. What does Jesus observe about the birds?

Look at the birds of the air; they do not sow or reap or store away in barns, and yet your heavenly Father feeds them.

—Matthew 6:26

This is a straightforward observation. We worry, but the birds don't. God feeds them, and he is going to feed us too. Jesus doesn't say "their" heavenly Father, but "your" heavenly Father. The same heavenly Father who cares for the birds cares for us. In observing the birds, the disciples ended up looking at themselves and recognizing their own fears and lack of faith. Observing a *kairos* event leads to examining ourselves.

When a *kairos* moment stops us in our tracks, this is the time to observe our reactions, our emotions, our thoughts. We must be honest in our observations. We have to see things as they really are if we are to change inwardly. This is not the time to look at how others have harmed us or insist that whatever happened is someone else's fault. It's not the time to say that what we've done is not as bad as what so-and-so did, or that no one was hurt, so it wasn't all that bad.

The Circle starts with honest observation. Look at it this way. You messed up. You said or did something to harm someone, or you didn't do what you should have to help someone. You know it. And God knows it. Why hide? Adam and Eve sinned against God and then hid. Did they really think they could fool the one who created their garden home in the first place? God knows all of our hiding places, and he is not shocked when we, in honesty, observe them.

Let's continue around the circle.

Reflect

Reflection starts when Jesus asks, "Are you not much more valuable than they?" (Matt. 6:26). Of course the answer to this rhetorical question is yes.

We were attending a church where one of the pastors had studied the LifeShapes principles. It was during a very difficult time in our marriage that we asked him to provide some counsel. Because of an extramarital affair, we found our family on the verge of disintegration. The pain of infidelity seemed impossible to work through but the one thing we knew was that we were committed to working through our issues and remaining together. We sat down with our pastor and talked for a long time. The pastor began by using the points of the Circle as a framework for us to address the problems in our marriage. In the process of reflection, we were able to discern kairos moments that had a significant impact on our relationship. With our pastor by our side, we went back through the process of Observe, Reflect, and Discuss for each of those kairos moments, thus beginning a cycle of learning and healing. In seemingly impossible situations, Jesus has given us a direct path toward his peace and his kingdom.

—A COUPLE IN CRISIS

Birds are valuable, but we are more valuable. Jesus helps the disciples put things in perspective. Asking questions is a good way to reflect.

So what do we reflect on? We reflect on our observations about the *kairos* moment that thrust us into the Circle. We ask ourselves why we reacted as we did, why we feel as we do, why this event brought these emotions to the surface. Once again our answers must be honest if real change is going to happen. (By the way, introverts will find this stage more natural than extroverts because it gives them opportunity to spend time alone reflecting.)

Reflection leads naturally to conversation and discussion.

Discuss

After observing and reflecting honestly, it's time to invite others into the process with us. "Who of you by worrying can add a single hour to his life?" (Matt. 6:27).

Matthew does not give us a verbatim record of the discussion between Jesus and his disciples at this point, but the usual teaching method in that day was question-and-answer. Discussion was a basic part of the learning experience. No doubt the disciples had some questions of their own.

Jesus was always prodding, always questioning, always saying, what about this and what about that? He pushed his disciples to look at things from a new angle, to gain a fresh perspective. We need to talk things over with others so that we reach clarity. Other people see things that we don't and challenge us in ways we are reluctant to challenge ourselves.

> Jesus says that the person who worries needs to change, not the things we worry about.

We try to change the things we worry about, but Jesus says that the person who worries needs to change, not the things we worry about. Change happens to us when we listen to questions and begin to try to answer them. "Why am I worrying about this when I know God is in control?"

God does not mean for us to live out our discipleship alone. We need others in our lives to share observations and reflections with, and who will be honest in their responses back to us. These people must be strong enough to handle your confession, be it small or large, and share God's grace and forgiveness with you. A trustworthy brother or sister will stand with you, pray with you, fight alongside of you, but he or she will not flatter you with empty words. "Therefore confess your sins to each other so that you may be healed" (James 5:16). ▲

▲ FOR MORE ON IN SEE THE TRIANGLE CHAPTER 10

Repentance is Not Easy

A young woman attended a Bible study in Arizona where we were sharing the Circle. She worked at a local bank and came to the study with a friend just for something to do. She was not a Christian, but she listened intently to what we had to say about *kairos* moments and the Circle.

One day when her till was counted out at the end of the day, it came up short. This young woman got into an argument with another employee about whose fault this was. She insisted that she had done everything the right way and that it was the other person's fault that the drawer came up short. The other employee was equally convinced that the problem lay with the young woman.

Money was missing, and something needed to be done. This young woman was experiencing a *kairos* moment.

She did go through the phases of repentance. After the argument with her coworker about who was responsible for the shortage, and once she had calmed down, she thought back through the situation. (Observe and Reflect.) She remembered some receipts she had not included in her ledger for that day—receipts that added up to the exact amount that was missing. It had been her fault after all. Then she took the next step—the hard one. She sought out her coworker and confessed her error. She was now halfway through the Circle.

Later, you will see how the bank teller did not simply stop halfway, but continued on through the Circle just as we must do. As Jesus continues his teachings in Matthew 7, he tells the crowd of the wise and foolish builders, basically saying, "Now some of you are wise, and some of you are foolish. The foolish ones are the people who listen to me. The wise ones are the ones who listen to me and act on the things they've heard. So, take action based on the changes that you want to see in your life." In moving from the Repent side of the Circle to the Believe side, we are taking action based on what we want our lives to look like, and we begin the true process of change in our lives.

CHAPTER 5

FAITH IS A FOUR-LETTER WORD

*E*xperience is the best teacher."

That may sound great when you say it, but it is almost always wrong. Just because we live through an experience—just because we go through a *kairos* moment—does not mean we have learned something from it, otherwise we would not have to repeat the same lessons over and over again. We learn by responding to the experience. In the same way, repenting by itself will not bring about change. Repentance is only the first part of the Circle. Stopping after we repent only invites the experience to recur and makes it harder to repent the next time.

After observing, reflecting, and discussing the situation with someone else—the process of repenting before God—we must move around to the left side of the Circle and begin to change our actions. How does this happen? Through faith. This is the second half of our Circle, the next process in the lifestyle of discipleship.

"Faith" says the writer of Hebrews, "is being sure of what we hope for and certain of what we do not see" (Heb. 11:1). Older translations use the word "substance"—faith is the substance of things unseen. Faith is not simply a nice idea; it is a substantive display of belief. It is being sure of something that you cannot see. Faith is not spelled r-i-s-k; It's spelled s-u-r-e! Faith is real stuff.

FAITH IS ACTIVE

The writer of James has some words that are sometimes hard for us to hear.

What good is it, my brothers, if a man claims to have faith but has no deeds? . . . faith without deeds is dead.

—James 2:14, 26

Faith is not like empty wishes or dreams that never come true. Faith is action. Faith is what takes us around the Circle and farther in our walk as disciples. Three principles of faith balance out the three principles of repentance. We discover these by continuing our study of the Sermon on the Mount.

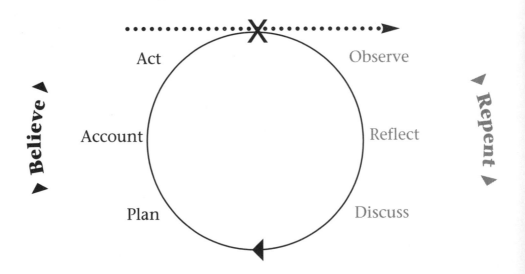

Plan

The first step in the faith response to a *kairos* moment is to Plan. On the basis of your observation, reflection, and discussion, you are ready to make a plan for inner change. Jesus says, "Look, you've got to have a different way of looking at your life, another way to deal with these issues. In fact, you've got to start thinking that there is another kind of plan that governs your life."

Ultimately *kairos* events lead us to discover we have used someone or something as a substitute for God. Planning involves seeking the kingdom of God first, no matter what the issue is.

> What do we do about building a life that is not based on worry, but on faith?

Suppose you have a bad habit that has escalated to the point of crisis. In reflecting on the cause, the Lord reveals an emptiness or void you are trying to fill by engaging that habit. What kind of plan do you need? A strategy for recognizing the feelings that lead you to embrace that behavior so you can react in a proper way. Suppose shopping is your habit, make a plan only to buy necessities and pay cash. Then let the Lord fill the emptiness. Or suppose God has shown you that you need to respond with more encouragement to a coworker; what kind of plan do you need? A specific plan for when and how you'll encourage your coworker.

But seek first his kingdom and his righteousness, and all these things will be given to you as well.

—Matthew 6:33

What do we do about building a life that is not based on worry, but on faith? Matthew 6:33 makes the clearest statement on planning in the Bible.

Planning is all about vision. We have a vision and we make a plan to get there, to make the vision happen, to make it come into being. If you have a vision for an afternoon on the beach, you put a plan into action and gather your beach chair, sunscreen, and big floppy hat. If you have a vision to save enough money for a down payment on a house, you make a plan for how much you will take out of each paycheck. We do this sort of thing all the time. Why not plan for the vision of God's kingdom?

Jesus tells us to make plans to seek his kingdom and his righteousness. Righteousness means right relationship. The rule of God in our lives becomes our vision as we let go of a worry-filled life. The worries of tomorrow no longer dominate us. God will take care of all things. This is the foundation of our planning.

Account

If a plan is to be effective, then we need at least one person to hold us accountable to it. It's pretty easy to cheat on a diet if no one else knows you're supposed to be on one. It doesn't take much to spend the down payment money on a weekend away if no one else knows you were saving for a house.

Jesus keeps us humble when he reminds us of our own frailties.

Do not judge, or you too will be judged. . . . Why do you look at the speck of sawdust in your brother's eye and play no attention to the plank in your own eye?
—Matthew 7:1, 3

We all know how easy it is to point out the mistakes or weaknesses of other people. We justify that whatever we have done is not nearly so foolish as what so-and-so did. We would never hurt anybody like that! How could she even consider that? What a jerk. Perhaps thinking—or saying—these things makes us feel better about ourselves, because we think we look better in comparison. We don't. That's the truth Jesus presses on us. Jesus tells us to do just the opposite—instead of calling other people to account for their actions, live in recognition that you yourself will be called to account. Hypocrites look for fault in others and miss their own faults. Jesus calls us to be authentic, not hypocritical.

Change doesn't happen in private. The repentance process that began internally becomes external through faith. You may be afraid to share with someone else because you think your thoughts or feelings are too private. This will only keep you from growing and changing. All the mistakes the heroes in the Bible made are public record for all time. Just think how Peter must feel about having people read and discuss how he denied Jesus three times!

> Jesus calls us to be authentic, not hypocritical.

When Jesus sent his disciples out, he sent them two-by-two. In pairs. In teams. In accountable teams.

Sharing your inner thoughts and outward failings with another person may be hard at first. Ultimately it is necessary for growth. The Circle will not turn if one spoke is broken or missing. We cannot skip accountability and still say we are disciples of Christ. It is that simple.

Act

Once you have a plan and an accountable relationship, the natural next step is action. Faith comes to the surface and produces action. Faith cannot be contained. Thoughts and intents that we hold within and do not act on are not faith, no matter what we might like to think. "My faith is personal" is a favorite. But that's a self-contradicting statement. Faith is always acted out, never kept bottled up.

When we were first married, my wife and I started attending St. Thomas' Church in England. As we learned about the Circle, it quickly became obvious how important its principles were to our marriage. We developed a plan to put the Circle into action as we thought about our marriage and life together. Now, several times a year, we schedule a weekend away together—with a flipchart. Together we look at the major events taking place in our lives, our *kairos* moments. We always go through the process of Observe, Reflect, and Discuss. We spend time talking about what has happened, how it has affected our lives as a couple, and what we can learn from it as we move into Plan, Account, and Act. By the time the weekend is over, we understand the impact of the *kairos* moments and we head back home with a plan for the future that strengthens our relationship

—A YOUNG HUSBAND

Let's revisit the story of the wise and foolish builders. Jesus tells the crowd about two men who were building houses. One builds on rock, the other on sand. Maybe you remember the old Sunday school song about what happens to the two houses when "the winds came up and rains came down." A familiar emphasis of this passage is on building our house—our life—on the solid rock of Jesus. Let's keep in mind all that has come before this story. Jesus has spent a significant amount of time teaching radical ideas. He has challenged his listeners to revolutionize their reactions to experiences that happen in their lives—some ordinary, some dramatic. What does Jesus want of his listeners? That they act on what they have heard. The wise man who built his house on the rock listened to what Jesus said and then *did what Jesus said to do.*

Remember the young woman at the bank? She had repented and come halfway around the Circle. Now she needed to believe and put faith into action.

Her first step was to make a plan. Her drawer came up short because she left out some receipts. So she came up with a better way to add up all of her day's activity. This plan would assure that she included everything that should go into the total. Then she spoke with the coworker she had blamed for the shortage. Together they agreed to check off each other's work to make sure everything was done accurately. As she did this, the young woman realized that she had changed. The *kairos* moment that set her in motion on the Circle had caused her to do her tasks better and, more importantly, to think differently about her coworker and herself.

SLINKY FAITH

Picture the Circle as a Slinky. You remember the children's toy, a spiral that winds round and round. I (Walt) was asked to speak at a retreat in the beautiful conference center in Lake Okoboji in Iowa. A woman attending the conference came to me the day after we talked about the Circle. She handed me a Slinky.

"This is for you," she said. "When you talked about disciples entering the Circle, I pictured it as a Slinky. We seem to just keep going around and around, but actually we are getting somewhere."

I keep the Slinky on my desk to remind me that in our journey of discipleship, we really are getting somewhere!

Once you are aware of the Circle—and put it into practice—your life can look like a Slinky, a series of loops held together by time. Each time around the Circle means you have grown a little more and taken on a little more of the character of Christ. Our lives really are about events connected together over time and our response to these events. The right response—Repent and Believe—leads us more fully into the kingdom. Skipping one or more of the spokes on the wheel means you will continue to struggle again and again with the same issue.

How do we take up the cross and become wholly devoted students following Jesus? Surrender to the process of change. Embrace the fruit of the Spirit God wants to grow in our lives. When it gets hard to face the issues of sin that surface in your life, push on through. Don't turn back and look for relief from the internal struggle. Persevere. The rewards will be great. Once you have tasted the goodness of the Lord, you will sell everything you have to keep it and know it more fully.

CHAPTER 6

THE GIFT OF WORK

*O*nce upon a time in a land faraway, the office opened at 8:00 AM. Cheerful, well-rested employees came to work and labored energetically all day. The office closed promptly at 5:00. The managers were pleased with the productivity of the employees. The employees straightened up their work areas and went home to have dinner with their families. The workday was over. Now it was time for rest and restoration.

Sound like a fairy tale? For many of us, this does not even remotely resemble our work life.

Back to our story.

After hundreds of years, travelers from the West brought with them shiny new inventions. They called them the computer and the Internet and the cell phone. The employees gathered around, punching numbers and clicking letters. What fun! The managers smiled. Productivity would soar! Now employees could work wherever they were.

Soon the employees were hunched over machines from early in the morning until late in the evening. Computer glare strained their eyes, and improperly arranged keyboards ruined their tendons. At the end of the day, they packed up their laptops only to plug them in again at home.

As they gathered around the coffee machine in the morning, one after the other bragged about how late they had worked the night before.

Now that sounds more like reality, right?

Our technological culture has evolved to a point where the number of hours you can work in a week is a major competition. When you drag yourself to work in the morning, can you moan to your coworkers that you were working until nearly midnight? Are you seen with your laptop in its case slung over your shoulder as you head home? Do you dial in to keep tabs on your messages when you're away from work? Do you take extra shifts to put some extra money on the mortgage? Do you find yourself involved in a different school or work activity every day of the week?

One father in a management position in a Christian organization routinely took his children to school in the morning and routinely went home for dinner with his family. When a coworker commended him for this, he confided that he had felt ostracized for many years because others thought he was not working as hard as they were.

What pushes us to work so hard and feel so proud about it? Something is not right here.

WORK COMES FROM GOD

Work is important. The very first command that God gives humans is to "be fruitful and increase in number" (Gen. 1:28). As appealing as snoozing in a hammock indefinitely may be, we were not created simply to exist. Adam and Eve lived in the middle of a garden, surrounded by all types of animals, birds, fish, trees, flowers, and edible plants. They were told to care for all of creation. What a job! They needed to be farmers, zoologists, botanists, ornithologists, and ichthyologists. Not only did they have to

keep these created beings alive, Adam and
Eve also had to establish an environment in which they could grow and
increase in number. This was work.

> Work is not part of
> the curse; it is what God
> designed us for.

Did you notice where in the time
sequence this command comes? It comes be-
fore Adam and Eve eat the forbidden fruit. It comes before sin enters the
world. It comes before Adam and Eve try to hide from their Maker. Work is
not part of the curse; it is what God designed us for. Clearly we are not to be
lazy and wicked servants; we were made to bear fruit.

But does this mean we are to be workaholics? In a word, no.

We all have stress in our lives, but it is not always bad stress. Stress, as we
recall from our high school physics class, is simply force applied to an object
to change its shape or course. Stress fractures occur when the object is un-
moving or unbending. The right amount of stress on a violin string creates
a beautiful note. Too little stress and you have a maddening buzz; too much
stress and you get a shrill off-key sound. We can't—and shouldn't—try to
avoid stress. It is part of life. But we are not made to bear too much stress.

Take a moment and answer the following questions:

- Do you regularly work six or seven days a week?
- Do you regularly work ten or more hours a day?
- Do you often work through lunch?
- Do you take work with you on vacation?
- Do you answer work-related e-mail or voice mail after you get
  home at night? On the weekend?
- Have you ever canceled a vacation because you had too much
  work to do?

- Do you think through work activities while eating with your family?
- Do you talk about your work more than your family while on a date with your spouse?

We could go on and on, but you get the picture. If you're a workaholic, you recognize yourself in these descriptions. But did you also know that workaholics are much more prone to stress-related diseases, mental and emotional fatigue, and problems in close relationships such as marriage?

This pressure-filled lifestyle is just as prevalent among Christians as in the general population. We may proclaim, "Cast all your anxiety on him because he cares for you," (1 Pet. 5:7) but we don't live it ourselves. We quote, "My yoke is easy and my burden is light" (Matt. 11:30), but we continue to pack heavy burdens on our backs. Something has gone very wrong.

This is not what God had in mind when he made us to be fruitful.

God designed us to be productive. But we misunderstand what that means. We build our identities around our activities. We have become human "doings" rather than human "beings." We've got the whole thing backward.

Rest   Work

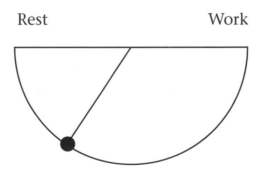

A biblical framework for a rhythm of life allows us to be fruitful in balance with being at rest. We need to be secure in who we are, based on what

When Mike first presented this teaching to our church staff, you could hear both sighs of relief and cries of pain. In a church of 12,000 members, the staff must split their time between running a large business and fostering an authentic community. Certainly a "normal" workweek isn't nearly enough time to accomplish both. Our culture has taught us that the only way to build a successful church is to build a large church. But in doing that, we had lost our focus on community. Then Mike comes in and tells us to reallocate our time, refocus our efforts on building disciples rather than building buildings. The staff's response revealed the level of pressure that they had been under, tears of joy and sorrow with one degree of separation between them.

— *WALT*

Christ did for us on the cross and the very great promises we have that we are loved and accepted by God. We must put the brakes on living a driven lifestyle so that we can gain the acceptance of others by what we do.

THE PENDULUM SWINGS

Scripture reveals the pattern of life that God created us for. We can see it in the lives of Adam and Eve before the Fall, and we see it lived out on a daily basis by Jesus. This is the pattern of life we call the Semi-Circle, so called from a picture of a pendulum swinging in a natural rhythm to and fro.

Then God said, "Let us make man in our image, in our likeness, and let them rule over the fish of the sea and the birds of the air, over the livestock, over all the earth, and over all the creatures that move along the ground." So God created man in his own image, in the image of God he created him; male and female he created them.

God blessed them and said to them, "Be fruitful and increase in number; fill the earth and subdue it. Rule over the fish of the sea and the birds of the air and over every living creature that moves on the ground."

Then God said, "I give you every seed-bearing plant on the face of the whole earth and every tree that has fruit with seed in it. They will be yours for food. And to all the beasts of the earth and all the birds of the air and all the creatures that move on the ground—everything that has the breath of life in it—I give every green plant for food." And it was so.

God saw all that he had made, and it was very good. And there was evening, and there was morning—the sixth day.

—Genesis 1:26–31

On the sixth day, God created humans in his image. "Image" brings to mind the idea of a reflection in a mirror or a portrait reflecting the likeness of someone. If a picture taken by a photographer shows a person's face, we say it is a good image or likeness of that person. When Moses first composed these words, however, there were no mirrors, no portrait painters, and no one-hour photo labs. In those days, a person would get a reference point for how he or she appeared by looking at others. But this is not the meaning of "image" in Genesis 1. A better word would be "imprint" or "impression." God left his handprint on us when he fashioned us from clay. We have an indentation on us that only the hand of God can fill. Yet from the Fall onward, we have been pulling away from the touch of our Creator, trying to fill the imprints with all sorts of insufficient fixes.

> God left his handprint on us when he fashioned us from clay.

Have you seen the memory foam mattresses? When you lie on the mattress, the imprint your body makes stays there for some time after you get up. The mattress remembers the impression your body makes. This is an impression that can only be filled with the body that made it. You can find memory pillows that remember the shape of your neck, even memory slippers that remember the impression of your feet and only yours.

We have an impression in our lives that can only be filled by the hand that made it. The difference is that the impression God puts on us never fades away.

Made to Work

Living a fruitful life is being like God, reflecting the image that is within us to be creators, to be makers, to produce something.

By the seventh day God had finished the work he had been doing; so on the seventh day he rested from all his work. . . . Then the LORD God took the man and put him in the Garden of Eden to work it and take care of it.

—Genesis 2:2, 15

Then the man and his wife heard the sound of the LORD God as he was walking in the garden in the cool of the day, and they hid from the LORD God among the trees of the garden. But the LORD God called to the man, "Where are you?"

—Genesis 3:8–9

In the cool of the evening, God walks in the garden he created. He wants the company of the crown of his creation, Adam and Eve. Remember, Adam and Eve have been working all day. Now God invites them to come away

> God gives them a daily reminder that his hand fills the imprint on each of them.

from their work and rest with him. These verses seem to indicate that this was a regular event, a routine in their daily lives. At the end of the day the Lord would turn up and expect his beloved ones to go on a stroll with him. God makes himself visible and audible each evening so Adam and Eve can feel connected to their Father. God gives them a daily reminder that his hand fills the imprint on each of them. This is how it was meant to be between the Creator and the created since the beginning of our time.

This time of retreat and rest following a day of labor was not an optional, "if you have time, but if not, don't worry about it" event. It was built into us as a natural part of our existence. It is how God created us to live.

But one evening our foreparents failed to show up. Adam and Eve had decided to go it alone that day, without the hand of God in their lives. God had given them instructions about living in the garden, but they chose to rewrite the instructions. They had sinned, and they knew it. Then they hid from the only hand that could fill them and make them complete.

After a confrontation with God, Adam and Eve are cursed to work among thorns and thistles, sweating in the heat from backbreaking labor. But this is not how it was supposed to be. Work itself is not a curse.

This leads us to several conclusions.

Unemployment causes our lives to fall below what is standard

When a person becomes unemployed, it's as though the person has fallen from the God-given call to lead a productive life. That's why people struggle so much when they lose their jobs. The focus of productivity and fruitfulness in their lives is lost; it's as though they stop being fully human. No wonder depression often accompanies unemployment.

There is no such thing as retirement

If you leave your job voluntarily, it will not be long before you feel the onset of depression. No amount of golf or fishing can take the place of being fruitful. And don't even get us started on sitting all day in front of the television. If you stop all productive activity in your life, you are pulling away from your God-designed calling. You cannot live a successful life as a human. Think we are out of line? Consider the people you have known or heard about who died within a year or two of retirement because they ceased to be fruitful.

There must be work in heaven

If you were counting on sitting in an endless praise and worship service, sorry. There was work before the Fall; therefore there must be work after the redemption. This life is a foreshadowing of the real life yet to come.

Work is a strategic part of human existence. We are to live productive lives or we will fall away from our God-given calling and the standard of basic humanity. We were created on the sixth day of creation in order to work. But more important is what happened on the seventh day.

CHAPTER 7

THE SEVENTH DAY

God created man and woman on the sixth day. He set them in a garden full of wild and wonderful creatures and delicious foods to eat. He gave them instruction on caring for the animals and plants in the garden. He told them to be fruitful. And he wasn't talking just about making babies.

But on the first full day of existence for Adam and Eve, God rested. And so did Adam and Eve. All of creation took a well-deserved break in activity. This was our first full day as humans—a day of rest. After a busy day of being created, the next thing we did was hang out with God for a whole day. Then the work began. We only have to go to the first page of the story to see that. From this we see an important principle of life: We are to work from our rest, not rest from our work.

> We are to work from our rest, not rest from our work.

TO AND FRO

Rest is God's healthy starting point for us. Remember, we are human beings, not human doings. God has established this order for us: rest, then work. But we have it backward. We pride ourselves on a strong work ethic, even using it as a sign of godliness.

Have you read Elijah's story lately? Here is a man who is the very definition of a prophetic ministry. He is the embodiment of the prophets. He is God's chosen mouthpiece during the reign of Ahab, one of the wickedest kings of Israel. So Elijah is not an insignificant character. He has plenty of work to do.

So to begin his amazing ministry, God sends Elijah to Ahab to say essentially, "It's going to stop raining for three years and it won't start again until I say so"(1 Kings 17). If someone said that to you, you'd think, "Ha, he's a nut case."

We can imagine that Elijah is now all set for a tough time. Ahab will resist, and Elijah will repeat his message and be God's man of the hour.

But that's not what happens. God says to Elijah, "Go and hide. I'll take care of you."

What? That's right. God sends Elijah for a season of rest before the main period of his prophetic work.

The true sign of godliness—imitating God—is to pattern our life after him. And for God, rest is vital. As a matter of fact, rest from our activities is listed in God's Top Ten. The Lord makes this perfectly clear. God says, "Don't kill." We say, "Okay, that's fair enough." He says, "Don't steal." We say, "All right, fine." He says, "Have a day off." We say, "What? You mean it's in there with all that big stuff?" The commandment to keep the Sabbath is right up there with "Don't kill, don't steal, and don't commit adultery." In other words, being a workaholic is, to God, just as bad as being a murderer or adulterer. Rest is not optional if we are to walk in the lifestyle of a disciple.

Since our first experience as created beings with our Creator was a day of rest, we must start from a place of rest to fulfill our calling to be fruitful.

Everyone knows how busy weekends can be, especially when you have three young children. There is always something that has to be done. Everything from sports to school plays, house cleaning to yard work, shopping to church activities, etc. With all of this activity, and the fact that I was working full-time during the week, I knew my children would never feel like they got an opportunity to just sit down and *be* with me. So, when they were young, I started to schedule breakfast dates with them. Each Saturday morning, I took one of them out for breakfast. This became part of the family rhythm for years to come as the children grew up. In the middle of relentless activity, we always found time to be together, to know each other and to learn from one another. This time has become so important to us over the years that I have no doubt my children will experience the same joy in rest with their kids as I have with them.

—A BUSY DAY

Resting in God—abiding in his presence—is the only way we can be successful in what he has called us to do.

When was the last time you scheduled a day of rest and relaxation on your calendar before anything else?

On the other hand, when was the last time you canceled a day of rest and relaxation in favor of a meeting or work task—or filled a day of rest with so many activities that it was no longer the least bit restful?

You face pressure to be successful in your job. You're involved in ministries through your church that you care about deeply. You're trying to build relationships with neighbors who are unbelievers. You want your own children to grow to be sincere disciples. You're running from soccer games to piano lessons to church board meetings.

> Rest is not optional if we are to walk in the lifestyle of a disciple.

You're busy with kingdom work! This is good; you are meant to be fruitful. Growth is a sign of life. But in order to be productive in the ways God wants you to be, you must live in the rhythm of the Semi-Circle.

FRUITFUL AND ABIDING

Imagine a pendulum swinging in rhythm—back and forth, to and fro. The shape created by this swinging pendulum is a semi-circle. At one end of the pendulum's arc is Fruitfulness. At the other end is Abiding. We can't have one without the other. We abide in Christ, then go forth to bear fruit. We bear fruit; then we are pruned back and enter a time of abiding. Rest. Work. Work. Rest.

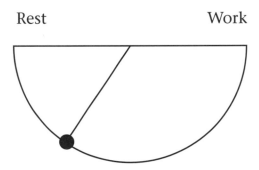

I am the true vine, and my Father is the gardener. He cuts off every branch in me that bears no fruit, while every branch that does bear fruit he prunes so that it will be even more fruitful. You are already clean because of the word I have spoken to you. Remain in me, and I will remain in you. No branch can bear fruit by itself; it must remain in the vine. Neither can you bear fruit unless you remain in me.

I am the vine; you are the branches. If a man remains in me and I in him, he will bear much fruit; apart from me you can do nothing. If anyone does not remain in me, he is like a branch that is thrown away and withers; such branches are picked up, thrown into the fire and burned. If you remain in me and my words remain in you, ask whatever you wish, and it will be given you. This is to my Father's glory, that you bear much fruit, showing yourselves to be my disciples.

—John 15:1–8

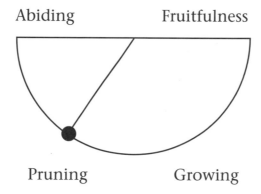

Abiding   Fruitfulness

Pruning   Growing

Fruitfulness happens in stages and seasons: abide, grow, bear fruit, prune, abide. This is the rhythm of the swinging pendulum, the Semi-Circle. It's really all about timing. We cannot bear fruit if we do not spend time abiding. But we cannot simply stay put in the Abide mode; a branch that does not eventually bear fruit will be cut off and cast into the fire.

Nowhere does this passage mention growth. Rather, growth seems to be a result of the right rhythm. Growth is not the same as bearing fruit. Sometimes we mistake spiritual growth for the fruit itself. This is not the case. We must grow before we can

> We cannot bear fruit if we do not spend time abiding.

My wife, Sally, and I had three young children and a teenage foster daughter. As if that weren't enough chaos, we lived and ministered in an area of inner-city London that had all the enormous needs associated with urban work. The church we led was going through a time of incredible pressure. In the midst of this, we made sure to carve out order and rhythm for the family. Sally set the table for breakfast the night before, and we ate all three meals together every day. Family mealtimes became points of retreat in times of battle; they were the place we could always come to abide.

—MIKE

see fruit. A newly planted apple tree, for instance, does not bear fruit for three years. Berry vines are pruned back intentionally and forced *not* to bear fruit for two to three years so that their root systems can be established. Growth must happen before fruit is produced. And growth comes from knowing how to abide.

PRUNING TIME

At the time of Jesus' incarnation, a vine would be cultivated and then planted and left to grow for three years before it was allowed to bear fruit. Every time it tried to bring forth a bunch of grapes, the gardener would cut it back. After the third year the grapes would be allowed to grow on their own. By then the branches were strong enough to support the weight of the grapes without breaking. After the harvest, the branches were pruned back for a time of nourishment and rest before the fruit-growing season began again.

Bearing fruit is the most natural thing in the world for a branch. It doesn't do it by straining to push out a grape. Looking at our lives, however, it would seem like producing fruit—making disciples—was strenuous. If fruit-bearing is not coming naturally in our lives, could it be that we have not spent the proper season abiding? Could it be that we are overgrown branches, too weak to support a single grape, let alone a bunch? Pruning is not the fun part of life. When is the last time you saw a church display a banner advertising "40 Days of Pruning," or heard about a small group studying "Pruning Yourself to a Better Life"? But if a grapevine is not pruned regularly, the branches grow spindly and weak. The branches need abiding time to gain their strength for the growing season.

> Aren't we supposed to be pressing forth with all of our energy to do the work of the kingdom? In a word, no.

We need to learn when it is our pruning time. This seems unproductive at first glance. After all, aren't we supposed to be pressing forth with all of our energy to do the work of the kingdom? In a word, no. We are supposed to pattern our life after Jesus. (We will look at scriptural examples of the Semi-Circle in the next chapter.) God is not impressed by our energy and determination; he wants to see us living in the manner he intends us to live, in a manner that will produce the fruit he intends us to bear.

Pruning is not automatic for the branch. Left on its own, the branch would continue to grow, increasing in size but decreasing in strength, endurance, and health until it would be unable to hold the fruit it was intended to bear.

From abiding we grow. From growing we bear fruit. From bearing fruit we are cut back. This is the pattern of the Semi-Circle. When the Lord is moving you into a time of pruning and abiding, surrender to him. You will find grace in the place of abiding and rest.

CHAPTER 8

FIND YOUR REST

*I*n the midst of our frenzied activities, it seems we are always trying to "schedule" a few minutes of rest. Or we work until we drop, then convince ourselves that we'll take a few hours off or even a whole day and be ready to plunge right back in. But is that the best way to rest? Or is that even rest at all? Could it be that because of our work habits we are becoming emotionally, physically, and spiritually drained human doings? At this rate, how fruitful are we ever truly going to be?

Jesus taught us something very different. Life—real, true, abundant life—only comes as a result of living in the natural rhythm with which we were created.

We use the Semi-Circle to help teach about the balance between rest and work because of the visual image of the swinging of a pendulum. There is a precise rhythm in that image that can help each of us find the best way to rest.

INTROVERT OR EXTROVERT?

What relaxes you? What gives you renewed energy?

Before you begin to practice the rhythm of the Semi-Circle, it is important to discover how you rest. We don't all rest in the same way. Recognizing whether you are an introvert or extrovert is the first step in learning how you rest. Introverts and extroverts are refreshed and energized by different types of rest.

Introverts and extroverts process information differently. For instance, extroverts think by talking. They cannot process information without bouncing their thoughts off another person. They love to brainstorm by thinking out loud. Extroverts will gladly ad-lib, speaking without notes for long periods of time. An extrovert's idea of a relaxing weekend would include entertaining friends, a party, or playing a rowdy game with lots of participants.

On the other hand, introverts process information internally. If you pass a new idea by introverts, they most likely will need a day or two to think about it before giving you any kind of feedback. They usually are the quiet ones in meetings or small groups as they sit and process what they hear. Introverts are often creative—writers, painters, composers—who come up with their best art in time spent alone. A relaxing weekend for an introvert might include pulling the blinds, renting a video or two, and selecting a good book to read.

> We find grace in being who God made us to be.

When it comes to knowing how to rest, understanding how God has created us makes all the difference. If you are an extrovert, don't expect to come away from a quiet evening spent by yourself all refreshed. You will pine for interaction with others, and may actually be more worn out from being without human contact. Of course, we are to set aside time to spend with the Lord alone. And as we get to know him more intimately, these times will be the most refreshing of all. But we find grace in being who God made us to be. If a cookout with friends is your way to relax, by all means fire up the grill. If you are an introvert, don't feel guilty saying "No" to the cookout invite. You know that the best way you can relax is to be by yourself for a time. Extreme extroverts and introverts are the farthest points on a continuum, and we each are at different points on the scale. It is important to find your point and discover the best way for you to rest.

RHYTHM AT ALL LEVELS

God's intention is for us to have rhythm at every level in our lives.

Days

Each day needs structure that enables you to rest and work, to invest in relationships and recreation. We need to work out a healthy pattern that matches our life's circumstances. Not everyone's circumstances are the same. As you work out your own structure, you'll find this framework is the order of your day. It's a great help to our personal discipline to maintain a balance of activity and abiding.

Weeks

The seven days of the week give the next level of rhythm. This will involve at least one day for rest and others for work. Our weekly routines should make way for special family members, church, and neighbors God calls us to love as ourselves.

Months

These longer periods give a broader opportunity to see the Semi-Circle in action. With period of several weeks or a month, you can stand back and begin to get the big picture of your life. Again, we must make a conscious effort to plan and establish biblical patterns of work and rest so that a dull routine does not take over. Schedule in regular times of celebration and retreat so you do not forget them.

When I was younger and still a single gal, I lived in a house with two other women—Deb and Terri. We were very close to each other and we valued the friendships that had formed among us. Terri is a nurse, and every six or eight weeks she worked a two-week rotation of night shifts. When this happened, the whole house went on night shift, so to speak. To make sure Terri didn't feel isolated during these times, Deb and I planned our meals around her schedule—even if that meant eating breakfast at four o'clock in the afternoon. We moved our life rhythms to fit hers. Also, everyone contributed to the grocery fund. Whatever was left at the end of month went toward a meal out together—another rhythm all three of us could count on to stay connected. None of these efforts required a lot of energy or even caused a substantial inconvenience. Yet, the impact of our decision was significant in helping us maintain deep and lasting friendships.

—JAMIE

Seasons

These are the phases of a year that enable us to rest for longer stretches of time or at regular intervals. God built seasons into his creation. We need to build similar seasons into our lives. Seasons include adolescence and adulthood; singleness and marriage; parenthood and empty-nesters. Some seasons, such as working at a new job or career, may require more of your time than others, such as working at a job you have been at for a number of years. In each of these seasons, you must find time to abide and work.

JESUS' RHYTHM

Jesus practiced a rhythm of life. He knew how to order his time to strike a balance between being with his Father and doing the work of the kingdom. Jesus is our example. As his disciples, we would do well to follow his example of abiding and fruit bearing.

Jesus rested through extended times of retreat

At once the Spirit sent him out into the desert, and he was in the desert forty days, being tempted by Satan. He was with the wild animals, and angels attended him.

—Mark 1:12–13

Jesus had just been baptized by John the Baptist. When he came up out of the water, the heavens tore open, and the Spirit settled on him like a dove. God said, "You are my Son, whom I love."

After that experience, you'd think Jesus was all set to launch his public ministry. After all, he'd been waiting around for 30 years already. Let's get on with it. But that's not what happened.

Before Jesus began his ministry, he went out into the desert for 40 days where he was tempted by Satan but made strong in the Spirit. He was alone, away from people, spending time with God. He knew exactly what he needed to do. He knew where he needed to start. Jesus spent time retreating with his Father. The very first thing Jesus did before beginning his ministry was to retreat.

Jesus came out of the desert full of the Holy Spirit. What does this say to us? We all need times of extended retreat, resting in the presence of God, focusing on him. Like Jesus, at the start of a new ministry or task or phase in our lives, we need to spend concentrated time receiving power and strength from the Father.

Jesus had regular daily times of quiet rest with the Lord

Very early in the morning, while it was still dark, Jesus got up, left the house and went off to a solitary place, where he prayed. Simon and his companions went to look for him, and when they found him, they exclaimed: "Everyone is looking for you!"

Jesus replied, "Let us go somewhere else—to the nearby villages—so I can preach there also. That is why I have come." So he traveled throughout Galilee, preaching in their synagogues and driving out demons.

—Mark 1:35–39

Jesus had finished a busy day of ministry, healing sick people, casting out demons—doing all kinds of amazing things. This was all done publicly, and the people were duly impressed. The next morning, people were already looking for him. They wanted to see more, hear more. We might think that this is the time to catch the next wave, keep going while the interest was high.

Let's not confuse Jesus' ministry with a presidential campaign. He was about to begin his second day of ministry. Despite the crowds that had already gathered, Jesus got up early to slip away. Jesus got up early in the morning to go to a solitary place to pray. Before doing anything else, before starting his day, he rested in the presence of his Father and talked with him.

Jesus taught his disciples about rest

The apostles gathered around Jesus and reported to him all they had done and taught. Then, because so many people were coming and going that they did not even have a chance to eat, he said to them, "Come with me by yourselves to a quiet place and get some rest." So they went away by themselves in a boat to a solitary place.

—Mark 6:30–32

When you look at the pattern of life the disciples began to develop, it's clear that Jesus was trying to teach them the same thing. In this passage, the disciples gathered around Jesus, reporting back to him all that they had done after returning from being sent out in Mark 6:7. So many people were coming and going that they didn't have a chance to eat. Jesus told his disciples to follow him to a quiet place where they could rest and eat. All this happened in the midst of what we would call revival. We might be tempted to "seize the day" and make the most of having crowds around. Instead, Jesus made rest a priority. We are to follow his lifestyle.

Consider your own lifestyle. Do you try to rest from work or work from rest? What do you do to sustain a rhythm of Abiding and Fruitfulness?

Jesus is the same yesterday, today, and tomorrow. That means he's doing the same things with us today as he did with his first disciples. He's teaching us. He's training us. He's helping us learn how to be like him. He's helping us learn to work from our rest.

CHAPTER 9

COME, WALK WITH US

Walking has rules?

Power walking does. You have to go at a certain minimum speed; you have to have one foot on the ground at all times; your arms have to swing just so in relationship to what your feet are doing.

Of course, not everyone power walks. Some people mall walk. The rules there are that you have to follow the outer shape of the mall and you can't stop to go in any of the stores.

Then there's the treadmill. To use a treadmill properly, you have to know your resting heart rate and calculate what your maximum heart rate should be according to your age and gender, and find the speed that gets you to that rate.

When did walking get to be such hard work?

When Jesus lived on earth, walking with the standard mode of transportation. When someone splurged on a vehicle, it was a donkey. When you walked with someone, you were sharing life together. You carried each other's loads, got to know one another, bonded.

So what is God's idea of a power walk?

What does the LORD require of you? To act justly and to love mercy and to walk humbly with your God.

—Micah 6:8

Here we have, in one verse, the summation of what God expects of us as followers of Jesus. It is a three-sided series of relationships: Up, In, and Out.

Out: "Do justly."

In: "Love mercy."

Up: "Walk humbly with your God."

Jesus, our compass on this journey, walked his life in three relationships. Up—with his Father. In—with his chosen followers. Out—with the hurting world around him. We see these three dimensions of his lifestyle in the following passage.

One of those days Jesus went out on a mountainside to pray, and spent the night praying to God. When the morning came, he called his disciples to him and chose twelve of them, whom he also designated apostles: Simon (whom he named Peter), his brother Andrew, James, John, Philip, Bartholomew, Matthew, Thomas, James son of Alphaeus, Simon who was called the Zealot, Judas son of James, and Judas Iscariot, who became a traitor.

He went down with them and stood on a level place. A large crowd of his disciples was there and a great number of people from all over Judea, from Jerusalem, and from the coast of Tyre and Sidon, who had come to hear him and to be healed of their diseases. Those troubled by evil spirits were cured, and the people all tried to touch him, because power was coming from him and healing them all.

Looking at his disciples, he said:

  "Blessed are you who are poor,

    for yours is the kingdom of God."

—Luke 6:12–20

Do you see the Up, In, and Out in this story from Jesus' life? Jesus began by praying, then called his disciples to him, then went down with them to the crowds who needed his touch.

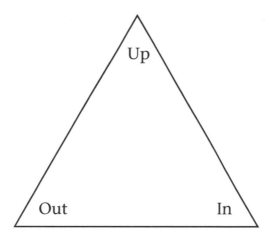

Having a relationship with other people—those we are close to, even those who are basically strangers to us—is something we can at least imagine. After all, we can see them and hear them; they are humans just like we are. But how do we have a real relationship with the Almighty God? How do we—in a real, practical sense—experience the Up relationship of the Triangle?

We walk. This is a whole different sort of power walk.

WALK HUMBLY WITH YOUR GOD

Walking with God illustrates the ideal relationship we can share with our Creator. Adam walks with God in the cool of the evening through the garden. Enoch walks with God, and is taken straight away to heaven. (Some have pictured this as God and Enoch walking along together, and God says to Enoch, "Look here—we're closer to my house than yours; let's just go to my place." Sounds good to us!) When Jesus calls his disciples, he invites them to walk with him. "Come, follow me" (Mark 1:17). Jesus is walking, and we are to walk with him.

Notice that Micah does not say, "*talk* humbly with your God." We have somehow boiled down the upward dimension of relationship to only talking and listening to God. If our relationship with another person, especially someone significant in our lives, were defined only by talking with that person, it would be a rather limited relationship. Time together and companionship matter.

The same holds true in our upward relationship with God. It needs to be more than just prayer time. We really need to live with him.

Jesus said he could do nothing by himself, only what he had seen the Father do (John 5:19). Jesus has observed the Father at work. How? By spending time with the Father. We can't see what another person is doing unless we are with that person. Jesus speaks in personal and intimate terms about his Father; the two were on very close terms. Jesus walked with his Father while here on earth. And now we have an invitation to walk with God the Father and Jesus ourselves.

When people wanted to get somewhere in the ancient world, they walked. And walking with someone meant spending time together. If you were a disciple with Jesus in those days, you spent much of your time walking on the dusty road with Jesus, talking along the way. You might stop at an inn for lunch and eat with Jesus. You would have shopped in the market with Jesus. When it rained, you would have huddled under a shelter with Jesus. In other words, you would have lived every part of your life with Jesus.

This is what we mean by following Jesus as his disciple. This is not a religious activity. It is not something you only do in church on Sundays. Jesus is a real, living person. Walking with him is a very real action. It involves every part of our life, not just our inner or "spiritual" nature. So as we explore the Up aspect of the Triangle, we are looking for very practical expressions of this relationship.

GOD CALLS, WE ANSWER

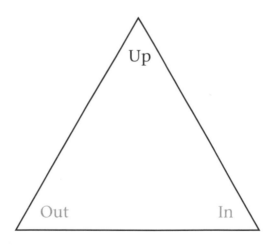

When you consider the Up relationship, keep in mind that you are not the instigator of the relationship. You do not have to work to keep the relationship alive. Every time you pray, you are simply responding to God's call to your heart. God is always the instigator in our relationship with him. Perhaps you feel burdened by some situation and you go to God in prayer.

Could it be that God started the series of circumstances rolling that led to you feeling loaded down and ultimately brought you to your knees? Of course it could. When we pray, we always are responding to God's call.

The same thing applies when we praise the Lord. We respond to events God has brought our way. When we give him gifts, we respond to the gifts he has given us. This is always the pattern: God initiates, we respond.

Most people, when they are honest, admit they have trouble keeping regular "quiet times" because of the craziness of life. A mother of young children who don't sleep through the night doesn't find it helpful when she's told to get up one hour before the rest of her household so she can have a quiet time. The husband taking care of a wife with Alzheimer's hardly dares close his eyes to pray over a meal, much less withdraw for 30 minutes of solitude. Some of us are in high gear so much of the time because of the legitimate demands of our lives that we hardly know how to go into low gear. We do need to make time to be with God. But this is not going to look the same for every person.

> Every time you pray, you are simply responding to God's call to your heart.

Why not have short, special times with God? Perhaps each morning as you walk out to the curb to pick up the newspaper or get the mail, you could make that a time you walk for just a moment with God. "How's it going, Father? Having a good day? I am. Although I've got to say, you've made it rather cold today." When you need a break from your desk, instead of heading downstairs to the vending machine, walk a couple of laps around the inside of your building and use the time to talk with God. When you're raking leaves, talk aloud to God. When you're rocking and nursing your baby in the middle of the night, be with God in the quietness. Turn the long commute you dread into a time to sing praises out loud.

If we truly are in relationship with him, wouldn't that include our "regular" life as well as those time we set aside as spiritual?

A young woman came up to me (Mike) a few years ago in some distress. She was having trouble finding time for prayer and Bible reading.

"Welcome to the club," I said. "Well done—you've spotted a problem many of us have."

"But what should I do?" she asked.

"Let's not think about 'quiet times' right now. Tell me, what do you like to do? What activity do you most enjoy doing?"

She answered, much to my surprise, "Canoeing. I love to go canoeing." I could have thought about this for a dozen years and I never would have guessed her favorite activity was to go out in a canoe. But I worked with this, and told her not to worry about praying or reading her Bible the next week.

"Instead," I suggested, "invite God canoeing with you this week. Let Jesus come with you in your boat."

When I saw her a few weeks later, she was beaming.

"I have had the greatest quiet times lately! Jesus and me in my canoe— it's great! And then it spills into the rest of the day. After we've gone canoeing, Jesus and I sometimes take a walk, or go shopping."

She gets it now.

A man would go to coffee with Jesus. He pulled up an extra chair to the table. He bought a coffee and a cream cake for himself, and would buy a cream cake for Jesus. He had only one complaint. Sometimes, he said, Jesus didn't want his cream cake. So the man would have to eat both of them.

He gets it. Life with Jesus can be just that personal.

You don't have to look far to find ways to invite Jesus into your everyday life. Walk with Jesus. Invite him to be a part of your everyday life. Let him accompany you as you drive, as you work, as you play.

PASSIONATE LIFE

GIFTS FOR THE GIFT-GIVER

How do you interact with other people during the day? You give time, you give gifts on special occasions or for no occasion at all, you do what you can to help someone who needs your help.

When you give yourself to the least, the lost, the hurting, the dying, you are interacting with Jesus. Feed the poor, provide shelter for the homeless, visit those in prison. Keep your eyes open to those who are in need. In the world we live in, this is not hard. We can find someone to help every day. It may be something small, like holding the door open at the store when a shopper comes out laden with bags. It may be giving a ride to a person who has run out of gas. Perhaps you could visit a shut-in. Jesus says when we do these activities, we are really giving to him. That is part of walking with God. This is the upward dimension in action.

Perhaps you have been so conditioned to think of God as a religious concept that you limit the time you spend with him to "religious times."

Gift-giving is a great way to strengthen a relationship. Give God a gift from your heart. Perhaps it will be a work of art you create just for him. (After all, he gives us gifts of art most every day—sunrises, sunsets, trees, mountains.) Maybe you will dance a dance or sing a song you wrote for him. The Scriptures are full of suggestions about giving gifts to God. We are to give him our best, not seconds or imperfections.

Give your time to God. You cannot have a deep, intimate relationship with someone if you do not spend time with that person. If you only give God a few minutes a day, maybe a couple of hours on Sunday, how intimately will you know him? Perhaps you have been so conditioned to think of God as a religious concept that you limit the time you spend with him to "religious times." What would happen if you started sharing your "regular" times with him? If you were to converse with God throughout the day, just chatting with him as you would with your spouse or with a close friend, can you imagine what that would do to your relationship with God? Maybe you could start making your "quiet times" with him truly quiet, where you and God simply sit together. Snuggling up to Jesus is a wonderful way to spend Up time with him.

If you ride a bicycle once, you don't claim to be an accomplished cyclist. Driving a car once does not make you an experienced driver—despite what teenagers may think! You cannot "get" something if you only do it once. Just as learning to ride a bike takes multiple attempts over time, walking with Jesus takes practice. Praying once does not mean you are walking in the Up relationship. It is important to develop a routine of talking with him during the routine of our day.

Walking is an amazing thing. Toddlers start off by sitting with their parents, watching them walk all over the place. Then they get the idea they want to try this new way of getting where they want to be. The first attempts are not so good. They fall a lot, maybe suffer some cuts and bruises. But they don't give up, do they? With practice, they are soon walking everywhere. They get the rhythm down, and in this rhythm they find that they no longer have to think about the mechanics of walking. They just do it.

The same thing happens as we practice walking with Jesus. At first, you may have to be reminded to walk with him. Maybe you post a note on the bathroom mirror saying, "Start day with prayer." Soon, however, you are greeting God as soon as you get up without having to be prompted. Practice

> Practice will get you into the rhythm of walking, and walking with God is the definition of discipleship.

will get you into the rhythm of walking, and walking with God is the definition of discipleship.

Our upward relationship with Jesus is how we abide in him. And, as we see in John 15, we (the branch) must abide in him (the vine) if we are to produce fruit.

All of our efforts are worthless if we do not have the Up relationship in our lives. We will be fruitless without abiding. When we abide, we cannot help but be fruitful. Once we secure our Up relationship with God, he begins to prepare us for the other relationships in our lives that he has called us to have. There is no other way.

FOR MORE ON ABIDING AND FRUITFULNESS, SEE THE SEMI-CIRCLE, CHAPTER 7

CHAPTER 10

GET INTO IT

*L*et's get personal. Do you have close friends in your life you can be completely open with?

Jesus was a social being. He had three close friends: Peter, James, and John. Then there were the other nine in his inner circle of friends, and then the wider circle of 72 followers. Jesus shared food with these friends, laughed with them, met their families—in other words, he "did life" with his chosen circle.

Jesus had an In relationship with his disciples.

God created us as social beings. We need close relationships. God made us to live out our faith alongside others. Life should come with a warning label: Do Not Attempt This By Yourself!

> Life should come with a warning label: Do Not Attempt This By Yourself!

How many people do you know who are in pain because they do not have a strong In aspect in their lives? In a world of technology that connects us to information at the click of a mouse and ever-increasing speeds, loneliness is becoming an epidemic.

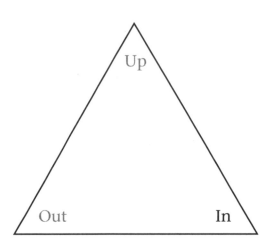

IN CHRIST

When God said it was not good for Adam to be alone, he wasn't just talking about marriage. God was relational with humans right from the start, and he means for us to be relational with each other. The theme of relationship runs through Scripture from beginning to end—it's the reason God planned for our redemption and promises us that we can be with him forever.

In order to fully grasp this relational concept, we need to understand what it meant to those who heard Jesus' teaching firsthand. A relationship was a covenant. In a covenant agreement, the stronger party confers equality on the weaker party. The stronger party invites the weaker party to a relationship of oneness. The entire Old Testament, telling the story of God's people before Christ, is based on a covenant between God and his people, Israel. God said, "I will walk among you and be your God, and you will be my people" (Lev. 26:12). God and his people are bonded together, inseparable.

The covenant implies that when the world looks at Israel, they will see God. So if God's people chase after other gods, the world will assume that the God of Israel is weak or doesn't even exist. Israel did run after other gods, sullying the covenant by becoming adulterers. God held up his end of the covenant. We humans are the ones who did not hold up our end of the bargain, and the result was a death sentence for all of us.

Scripture reminds us constantly that God wants to have a relationship with us. And relationship is much more than a contract. Relationship is a gracious commitment, fully identifying with one another, sharing all possessions, being loyal no matter the cost. This relationship is expressed in the very nature of God becoming incarnate.

Jesus entered our world to establish a new covenant. He invites us to live in his kingdom in a covenant relationship with him. We are one with Jesus, bonded to him and inseparable. Jesus says that we can now do all that he has done and more, because we are now in a relationship with the king himself. (See Luke 22:29–30.)

We are now "in Christ, " a favorite phrase of the Apostle Paul in his letters to New Testament churches. For Paul this is shorthand for the covenant relationship that God has with his people.

But now in Christ Jesus you who once were far away have been brought near through the blood of Christ.

—Ephesians 2:13

In the ancient world (and in some societies still today), the act of establishing a covenant was based on receiving and giving. In the first century, if you went to another person's house and he offered you a meal, you would then look to reciprocate and give something back. This was an entry-level covenant, which then would increase as the two parties received and gave time, money and possessions to one another.

Entering into a covenant is not something to take lightly.

Jesus selected 12 people specifically so he could be with them, spend time with them, build strong relationships with them over the three years that they spent together in his public ministry.

Jesus commenced his relationship with Peter, James and John with an entry-level covenant. Jesus received the use of their boat as a platform to preach from. When he finished, he gave the fisherman a gift of fish (Luke 5:1–10). The relationship between Jesus and these three men continued to grow to the point that Jesus gave the ultimate gift—his life. And he told his followers that once they received this gift, they would need to continue in the covenant by taking up their crosses—in other words, by giving their lives as well.

The early disciples, just as we do today, had trouble grasping what being in a covenant with one another really meant. During the Last Supper, they argued about who would be the leader among them.

Also a dispute arose among them as to which of them was considered to be greatest. Jesus said to them, "The kings of the Gentiles lord it over them; and those who exercise authority over them call themselves Benefactors. But you are not to be like that. Instead the greatest among you should be like the youngest, and the one who rules like the one who serves."

—Luke 22:24–26

We're a long way from the culture of the first century, so once again we must remind ourselves what Jesus' listeners understood. When we think of being a Christian servant, we think of voluntarily giving our time, our efforts, our possessions to others. But in Jesus' time, this would have been the role of a benefactor—the very thing Jesus told his disciples they were *not* to be. Servants were those who had no possessions. Their time and activities were not their own. Servants had nothing to give. All they could do in a covenant relationship was receive. Jesus tells us to become the servant, not the benefactor.

LIVING IN LOVE

In order to build true, biblical relationships, we must learn how to receive. While we tend to be pretty good at "getting" things for ourselves, we're not always so good at graciously receiving from someone else. If you broke your foot and had to depend on other people for just about everything, how would you feel? A lot of us would have real trouble with that. We would have to receive the care and generosity of others instead of taking care of ourselves and not needing anyone else. But remember, servants receive.

Once we receive, we reciprocate by being the giver so the other person can be the servant and receive. This is the basis of covenantal life—receiving and giving.

We are thousands of years away from the ancient world. So what does living in covenant relationships look like today?

You meet someone in a small group, a Bible study or your church service. You are both believers. This person invites you out for coffee, and you accept. At the end of that time together, you suggest having dinner together the next week. Following dinner, your friend compliments your lasagna, and you

> Giving and receiving are the foundation of an In relationship.

hristmas can be a *kairos* moment for many people; my wife Sue and I were no exception. One Christmas past, as Sue surveyed the gifts under the tree—she observed that all the gifts she had bought for me were beautifully wrapped and creatively presented. Yet, my gifts for her were either unwrapped or simply in the shopping bags that I brought them home in. Sue was upset by my lack of effort and apparent lack of love expressed through these negligent actions.

But this situation was way over the top of my head, I didn't understand where Sue was coming from. She finally brought up the topic one evening and as we talked through the situation, we realized we had inevitably been influenced by the experiences and expectations of our formative years. This led to a deeper discussion on how we express our love for one another and how we receive love from each other. Instead of letting our differences result in hurt and conflict, we were able to make a plan in which we could appreciate one another's differences and make an effort to express love in ways that each of us could truly appreciate.

—NIGEL

give her the recipe. She offers to have your son over for an afternoon while you do some errands. You help her wallpaper her entryway. As this covenant relationship builds, you are "doing life" together. You find it natural to share intimate matters of your heart. When your friend offers to pray with you, you receive. Giving and receiving are the foundation of an In relationship.

Jesus is our compass, and we are to follow his lead in the area of covenantal relationships with one another. This inward relationship—living in love with one another—is the only identifying mark Jesus said Christians were to have:

L ifeShapes helped us move from building a great congregation to transforming the community. Our focus was no longer building bigger buildings or implementing as many programs as we could. It became a shift centered on how we could reach the community. How each member of our congregation could focus on building a few meaningful and authentic relationships that would make a true difference in their daily lives. LifeShapes, especially the Triangle, provided the tools for teaching us how to make that leap with very little effort.

—WALT

By this all men will know you are my disciples, if you love one another.

—John 13:35

Jesus had people who were close to him. God wants the same for us. Jesus did not send out the disciples to do kingdom work alone; he sent them in pairs. Even when Jesus sent for a donkey, he sent two disciples to lead the animal to him. Think about that!

The staff of the church I (Mike) served in Sheffield, England, worked hard on this In dimension of relationships. After a few years, people noticed. They commented that the whole culture of the church had changed. What made the difference? The staff met together once a month just to have fun. That's it. No Bible study. No prayer. No sermon. No agenda. Just people having fun together and building relationships. Out of those In relationships grew the times of intimacy that are the bedrock of close friendship. People noticed, and the benefits spilled over to many others.

People leave churches all the time because they don't feel connected. They may be serving on half a dozen committees or ministry teams, but they don't have the In relationships that go beyond the boundaries of the work the committee does together. Churches sometimes do very well with the Up dimension—worshiping God together—and the Out dimension—serving the community around them, but not so well with the In dimension. People feel this lack of balance and move on in search of intimacy. The community of God should be the place they find it.

When we ignore the call of Jesus to do life together, we suffer.

Walking with Jesus is not an easy stroll through life. It is not a religious feeling. It is a practical, daily experience of living in the kingdom of God, where the way of life is different from what we have always been taught. But it is the way of true life. Unfortunately, many Christians choose to blunder around this world, ignoring the call of Jesus to follow him as a disciple. When we ignore the call of Jesus to do life together, we suffer. When we don't have the In aspect of the Triangle in proper focus, we are not living in proper relational balance.

Are you walking as a disciple with a few others who can encourage you and hold you accountable, or are you going it alone? Even the Lone Ranger had the faithful Tonto as his partner. Who can walk alongside you?

CHAPTER 11

OUT WITH IT

*S*ecure a balloon to a faucet; turn on the water, and what happens? As the water enters the balloon, it will slowly expand and take on its designed shape. As long as the water continues to flow into the balloon, the balloon will continue to inflate and fill with water. But at some point the balloon will get too full—it has to let out some water or burst. Now, if you give the balloon several small outlets, that balloon can continue to take in water from the faucet. The balloon can remain full, benefit from a continuous supply of fresh water and still give out water.

The principles of the Triangle are like that balloon. UP—You hook up to God and he fills you with his presence, his power, and his purpose. IN—As God fills you, you grow, enabling you to fulfill your ministry within the community of believers. But you can't stop there! Jesus has called his followers to a three dimensional life so to remain healthy and vital and available to receive even more of God, you also have to let God's presence flow OUT from you to those around you.

You **receive** from God;
You **share** together what God has given;
You **give** to others what you have.
That is how you live a balanced life.

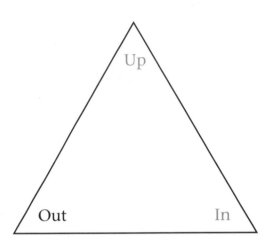

IF IT'S SO EASY, WHY IS IT SO HARD?

Most Christians eagerly will practice the Up dimension of relationship. And on an individual basis most are willing to reach out to those within their close circle, the In dimension. But the thought of leaving our safe environment and entering the world of the lonely, the needy, the dying is scary stuff.

If the word evangelism sends chills down your spine, join the club. Many Christians feel the same way. Much of our attitude has to do with a misunderstanding of what evangelism really is. We know we are called to share the gospel and we feel guilty when we don't. So we encourage our churches or those within our churches who have the 'gift' of evangelism to do our Out for us—as if we could find balance by proxy. How do we reconcile our fears and failures with evangelism to the call of Jesus to "go and make disciples?"

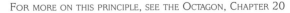

 FOR MORE ON THIS PRINCIPLE, SEE THE OCTAGON, CHAPTER 20

Our world needs relationships, and God wants us to reach out and build them. A young mother feels totally lost as she spends day after day at home alone with her three preschoolers. Your neighbor down the street confesses that he is having an affair and is planning on leaving his "loveless" marriage. The clerk at the grocery store seems distracted and sad. A young college student spends his first Sunday in a new city and he walks through the doors of your church.

Then Jesus made a circuit of all the towns and villages. He taught in their meeting places, reported on kingdom news, and healed their diseased bodies, healed their bruised and hurt lives. When he looked out over the crowds, his heart broke. So confused and aimless they were, like sheep with no shepherd. "What a huge harvest!" he said to his disciples. "How few workers! On your knees and pray for harvest hands!"

—Matthew 9:35-38, *The Message*

Jesus had a reason for coming (Mark 1:38) and it wasn't to build churches. We all know people who are confused and aimless, sheep with no shepherd. We who know the shepherd, we who know his consuming, unfailing love for us, are to go out and harvest the lost. Our work is to bring them into the safe haven of community with God and with his followers.

Once we understand Jesus' strategy of outward relationships, our fear often vanishes. We are encouraged to look for people we naturally connect with and build relationships with them. Once a relationship is established, sharing the

> Once a relationship is established, sharing the message of the Gospel can come easily.

message of the Gospel can come easily. God accepts the responsibility of preparing the harvest. All we are doing is making a connection with a person whom God has already prepared.

KEEPING THE BALANCE

If you talk to the average person, you'll find most people are good at two out of the three dimensions. They're all Up and Out, or all Up and In. Sometimes we're even all In and Out without much talking to God going on. Life is busy, lots to do at work, lots of places to be with the family. So we just sort of glance upward and think, "I hope everything's okay up there." It's really hard for us to keep all three relationships in balance.

Perhaps you're in a small group, so you think you've got the right balance of relationships. Small groups take on their own personalities, and they also tend to do well with two out of the three dimensions just like individuals. Imagine having a conversation like this one with yourself:

"There doesn't seem to be as much life in our group as there used to be."

"What do you do with your time together?"

"Well, we worship and we sing and we read Scripture together. And we spend a lot of time sharing our lives and praying for one another."

"Do you ever engage with anybody outside the group? Do you go and serve anybody or clean up an old lady's yard or just go and knock on some neighbors' doors and say, 'How can we pray for you?'"

"No, we don't do anything like that."

"That explains why you feel flat. Your group is getting two-dimensional."

FOR MORE ON EVANGELISM, SEE THE OCTAGON, CHAPTER 23

Our Worship Team was struggling. We had made UP the focus of our practice times when what we really needed was IN—more time to relate to and encourage one another. But even after we got that sorted out, something was still missing. We needed an OUT and providing a worship experience for the church on Sundays didn't count.

We were in the midst of one of the hottest summers on record so we decided to buy a couple of cases of soda and hand them out to people stuck in late afternoon traffic. On each can, we stuck a label that simple said "Thought you might be thirsty—here is an expression of God's love in a practical way, no strings attached!" The response was open and positive. Afterwards, encouraging stories drifted in from the community. Although we may never know the full impact of our effort. But the effect of balancing UP, IN, and OUT for our team was incredibly enriching.

—A WORSHIP TEAM LEADER

Another group might pray together and go out on the streets with the Gospel, taking the message of Jesus to the rough and tough. But they don't spend time on the needs of their own group. This group is also two-dimensional.

Do you see how it works? It's really simple. And of course the simplicity means that most people say, "Well, I already knew that." Okay, then, if you knew it, why aren't you doing it?

GONE FISHIN'

Jesus said he would make us fishers of men. The method of catching fish in Jesus' day was to bait the water, then spread a net to gather as many fish from that bait as possible. Of course, this required that the fisherman first go to where the fish were. If they didn't find fish in the first place they threw their nets, then rowed over to a new spot and looked for fish there. If we simply stay in our safe zones—our churches, our small groups, our Christian sub-culture—we will not be where the lost are. We have to get out of our comfortable settings where there are people who do not yet know that God loves them so much, he cannot stop thinking about them.

How many non-Christians do you have a relationship with? How many unbelievers can you call "friend?" What is keeping you from reaching out to the people God has already placed in your life? If you are truly serious about following the Master, you need to be willing to go where he would go and reach out to the same people he came to minister to.

Over and over again in the Gospels, we see the three-dimensional life of Jesus. He habitually took time to be alone with his Father. He invested heavily in a small group of people as close friends and coworkers for the kingdom. Having prayed (Up) and gathered these friends (In), Jesus then moved (Out) into the crowd and did the work of the kingdom—proclaiming the Good News, challenging injustice, teaching the people, healing the sick and meeting needs of all kinds.

God made us to live in three dimensions. Jesus lived in three dimensions. We can't improve on that. Are you living in three dimensions?

CHAPTER 12

LEADERS AND LEARNERS

*L*et's pause to make sure we're still on the same page. Jesus, the wisest man ever to walk the earth, taught his disciples to live in a kingdom community. Simple shapes help us remember the principles he taught.

A disciple uses memorable moments in life—*kairos* moments—to enter a circle of repentance and faith. This circle continually spirals closer and closer to the heart of Jesus. The Circle is the life of discipleship in a nutshell.

God created us to be fruitful. But fruit only comes if we live in a gentle swing between rest and work, with seasons of abiding, pruning, and fruit-bearing. God's plan is that we work from our place of rest, not rest from our work. Our life in God makes us like trees planted by streams of water, bearing fruit in season. This is the Semi-Circle, the balanced life. Disciples must have balance between rest and work.

We also need to have the proper relational balance in our lives. The right mix of Up (our relationship with God), In (relationships with fellow followers of Jesus) and Out (relationships with those outside of the faith) makes up the Triangle. As we receive grace from God, we pass it on to those with whom we have relationships. When these relationships are not in the right proportion, we wobble in all three.

The Circle ⬤ , the Semi-Circle ◗ , and the Triangle ▲ : Each of these shapes reflects an aspect of discipleship that Jesus taught and lived out. We cannot improve on Jesus. We need to listen to what he is still saying today and obey by following him with all of our hearts and all of our lives. This is not a religious exercise or experience. Following Jesus is a very real, nuts-and-bolts action and attitude that shapes every area of life.

We want to make this clear: we are not talking about part of your life. We are not talking about just your religious practices or charitable moments. Jesus wants *all* of you—your time, talents, money, experience, interests, inabilities and failures. And he does not call only professional ministers or "super saints" to be his disciples. He looks at each of his sons and daughters and issues this call: "Follow me."

Following Jesus is all about relationships. All of Scripture is about relationships. And we are all called into this lifelong walk with God. The first three shapes, no doubt, are easy to fit into your idea of what every disciple should practice. The next two shapes—the Square and the Pentagon—may be seem a little less obvious in how they apply to your everyday life. You might think that they apply only to specially gifted Christians. We assure you that everyone who is a follower of Jesus must learn the principles of these two shapes as well. Are you ready to continue our journey?

ME, A LEADER?

A quick browse through the shelves of a library or an Internet search reveals more theories about leadership than any of us could sort out and understand. Even the word puts us off sometimes. We're disillusioned with "leadership" in every form—from the church board to the workplace to the national government. And most of us don't see ourselves as leaders. We're content to hold our place in the masses and not have to be responsible for the kinds of decisions leaders make.

Only one leadership theory truly matters. What does Jesus teach us about leadership?

We're all leaders, whether we realize it or not. Parents lead children. Teachers lead students. Employers lead employees. Small group facilitators lead those who attend the group. Older people lead younger people. Friends lead friends. We all look like sheep from the front, but shepherds from the back. In other words, someone is looking to you to lead, and you are looking to someone to lead you. It's part of our relational nature.

> We're all leaders, whether we realize it or not.

After the resurrection and before going to heaven, Jesus told his followers to go out into the world and make disciples. This word, *mathetes*, means "learner." Jesus wanted the Twelve to make learners, to help people learn what it means to live in the kingdom of God. He wants us to do the same.

The call to go and make disciples is a call for leaders. It doesn't mean all of us have to be international evangelists. It does mean that we need to be ready to lead in individual relationships when the opportunity comes. So that we can be as effective as possible, we look at how Jesus taught his disciples to be leaders to the learners around them.

THE ORIGINAL SERVANT LEADERSHIP

Following Jesus' model of discipleship will mean acting in ways that make us unpopular with the culture around us. This has always been the case of those who follow Jesus. There's a lot criticism these days about leadership. Typically it comes from those who don't like being under authority. Thus, they tell others in authority how they ought to function. Jesus experienced this attitude firsthand.

Then James and John, the sons of Zebedee, came to him. "Teacher," they said, "we want you to do for us whatever we ask."

"What do you want me to do for you?" he asked.

They replied, "Let one of us sit at your right and the other at your left in your glory."

. . . When the ten heard about this, they became indignant with James and John. Jesus called them together and said, "You know that those who are regarded as rulers of the Gentiles lord it over them, and their high officials exercise authority over them. Not so with you. Instead, whoever wants to become great among you must be your servant, and whoever wants to be first must be slave of all. For even the Son of Man did not come to be served, but to serve, and to give his life as a ransom for many."

—Mark 10:35–37, 41–45

Jesus sets the default position for all leaders to pattern themselves after.

Let's face it. If you are a leader and people in your group tell you that they want you to do whatever they say, you laugh. Or indignation stirs up as you say, "Who do you think you are?" Parents do this, teachers do this, employers do this.

But not Jesus. Rather than expressing amusement or indignation, Jesus seizes a teachable moment. Jesus is infinitely patient. In this passage, Jesus sets the default position for all leaders to pattern themselves after. Leaders are to be servants. And, as we saw when studying the Triangle, a servant is not one who gives—because servants have nothing to offer. Servants must first receive before they are able to give. As servants of God, we have nothing in our hands except what God places there. When we recognize that we are servants with nothing to give, we understand that a leader in the pattern of Jesus must rely on grace at all times. Grace is receiving what we don't deserve and cannot attain on our own. If we need grace, it is because we recognize we are empty—the very sign of a servant.

Just how did Jesus model servant leadership? He did it by:

- Telling his disciples, "You don't know what is best for you, but I do. So just do what I tell you to do."
- Stepping into the line of fire; taking the shots fired at those he led.
- Washing the feet of the disciples, thus removing the grime and filth that was part of their lives.
- Leading in a clear and visionary manner.
- Calling Peter, one of his closest friends, "Satan" because Peter was speaking from his flesh and not his spirit.
- Braiding together strands of rope to whip those who bought and sold in his Father's house.

Can you see that the kind of "servant leadership" that Jesus taught and demonstrated goes against the grain of what we normally think of when we hear the term? At times, servant leadership is a difficult and lonely road to walk.

A shepherd sometimes needs to use a crook to snag a sheep around the neck and drag it back into the safety of the fold.

A shepherd sometimes needs to use a crook to snag a sheep around the neck and drag it back into the safety of the fold. It may not be comfortable for the sheep at the time, but it sure beats getting eaten by a wolf. Servant leadership means knowing what to do—beyond offering sympathy—when someone you know has lost his or her way. Jesus prepared his disciples for that kind of leadership.

Human nature has not changed in two thousand years. This is why we can still follow the leadership practices of Jesus today and expect the same results Jesus saw. We say "leadership practices" because Jesus had several different styles of leadership, thus making himself a more effective leader. In the next two chapters, we will look at four stages of discipleship and the styles of leadership that are most effective during each stage. This process will take us around a square that transforms us from being learners to being leaders.

CHAPTER 13

LEARNING REALITIES

We use a square to teach about leadership because we can see Jesus' leadership style in four stages. Each side of the Square leads to the next, creating a cycle of leadership.

Let's begin by looking at the first two stages of learning to which leaders must be ready to respond. If disciples do not get through these two stages, the square will never be complete.

STAGE 1

Disciples are confident and incompetent.
Leaders are direct and set an example.

The time has come, he said. "The kingdom of God is near. Repent and believe the good news!"

As Jesus walked beside the Sea of Galilee, he saw Simon and his brother Andrew casting a net into the lake, for they were fishermen. "Come, follow me," Jesus said, "and I will make you fishers of men." At once they left their nets and followed him.

When he had gone a little farther, he saw James son of Zebedee and his brother John in a boat, preparing their nets. Without delay he called them, and they left their father Zebedee in the boat with the hired men and followed him.

—Mark 1:15–20

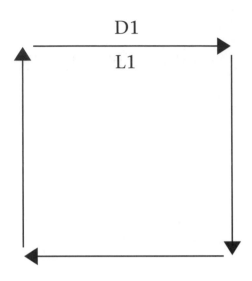

Jesus simply says to the fisherman, "Come, follow." They step out, put down their nets, and follow him. Somehow they are confident in his leadership, confident enough to follow. Their confidence, however, is rooted in their enthusiasm at having been chosen, not in experience or any real knowledge about what they are getting into. They have no clue. None whatsoever. If they are at all scared, they muster the confidence to start the journey anyway. We might wonder whether they would have started this journey if they had had any realistic picture of what it would be like. But they didn't, so they were confident and enthusiastic.

Into that situation, Jesus speaks directly. He is the one giving the instructions. His directness draws the fishermen in. Jesus is also assertive. He did not begin with consensus-style leadership. Finding out what these fishermen thought about living in the kingdom of God was not on his agenda. He did not say, "Guys, I've got this idea about the kingdom. Maybe I could try it out on you and see what you think." He did not try to get any of these fishermen to agree with his strategy and tactics. He did not call for a vote on his teaching of the kingdom. If he had, the whole matter would probably still be in committee discussions! He simply said, "Come, follow me, and I will make you fishers of men." This is clear, directive, assertive language. We'll see that later in his ministry, Jesus used a different tone, but at this stage of the disciples' experience, direct leadership is what they needed.

Jesus led by example in this early stage. He went about the land preaching, healing, casting out demons. Along the way he offered very little explanation to those who witnessed him at work. The disciples just followed along, watching and observing it all. They listened to all he said, but had very little understanding.

Do you remember your first day in college? "This is great. I'm really doing the adult thing now." Or your first job? "I'm going to go in there and show everybody I know exactly what I'm doing." Or your first time as a parent? Your own baby! No doubt you were excited—leading to confidence. You felt ready to take on the world—or at least a little baby.

Soon, however, you began to feel the lack of experience and competence. What do you do when you're exhausted from trying to prepare for two papers and three exams in one week? What do you do when that baby won't stop crying? Enthusiasm will only take you so far, so you call your mother or someone else who knows how to calm a baby.

The leadership style that speaks to the needs of this stage is directive. The leader gives clear instructions and sets an example, modeling behaviors and expectations for learners. This is not the time for seeking consensus or prolonged explanations to justify a leader's decision.

Have you ever taught a child how to ride a bicycle? That kid is raring to go. He thinks he can just hop up onto that seat and peddle away. But you know better, because you've fallen off a bicycle a time or two. So you make sure you've got eye contact and give some basic instructions—mostly saying, "Just listen to me and do what I say."

When you are leading someone through a learning cycle, be it a mentoring a new disciple, training a new employee, welcoming a new member to your small group or potty training your toddler, directive leadership works well during this period of adjustment and orientation. This means announcing a clear direction and walking confidently, not being pushy or unpleasant. The disciples are enthusiastic and want to do the right thing. The example to follow must be clear and consistent.

When initiating any new project or learning cycle, the leader needs to clearly set out the vision God has given. This vision gathers the disciples; it sifts out those who don't respond to the vision and motivates those who do, even though they may lack experience and competence at this stage. Any consensus approach at this stage dilutes the vision. Then you will lack the focus and motivation to carry through. You probably wouldn't ask the seven year old how he thinks you should go about teaching him to ride a bike. Even if we are not used to directive leadership, we need to recognize it as entirely appropriate at this stage and welcome it.

This poses a problem for some people. We are suspicious of directive leadership. We have a legacy within recent memory of directive leaders who have been tyrants, who have manipulated their followers' lives for evil intents. Also, our western independent mindset automatically questions directive authority. We live in a democratic society where everyone gets to vote—whether they understand the issues or not—and we think we need to carry this through in everything we do.

Yet when we start out on a new trail, we need a strong, confident leader to show us the way. We like to have someone with us who knows where he or she is going, someone who knows where the rough spots are and how to get around them. If you are to lead as Jesus did, you must do so with firmness and confidence. Jesus started with the kind of confidence and directness we often lack.

When we start out on a new trail, we need a strong, confident leader to show us the way.

Children have the universal experience of asking why? they have to do something they don't want to do and getting the answer, "Because I said so." The parent in this situation is not taking an arbitrary or tyrannical stance. The simple truth of the matter is that the parent knows best; the parent understands factors that the child cannot fathom. In some circumstances, the parent cannot offer an explanation that the child can understand. At that moment, the child has to trust the parent to know best.

Resist the urge to endlessly explain what you are doing or get feedback from those following. Lay out your plan and stick with it.

This is why Jesus said that leaders must be broken, humble servants. If you start out as a direct leader, but are not humble, you will soon find you are walking alone. Remember that as a leader you are simply a representative of the Great Leader himself.

STAGE 2

Disciples are unenthusiastic and incompetent.
Leaders become coaches.

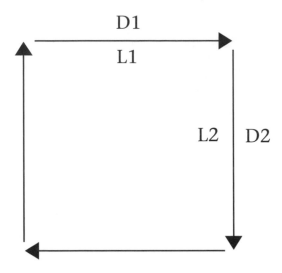

So you're trotting along the sidewalk hanging on to the back of the bicycle seat. The child is pedaling away. The handlebars are wobbling all over the place, but he's got the pedaling thing down. He says, "Let go!"

Do you?

You know what's going to happen. You know the child is not ready to ride alone. But he insists, and he pedals so fast you soon have no choice. The bicycle seat slides out of your grip.

The next moment the bicycle tumbles, and the child is looking up at you with a scraped knee wondering what in the world happened. Why did you let go? This is not fun.

Eventually Jesus' disciples become aware that they really have no idea what they are doing. Reality sets in. The fun starts to fade away for the disciples. The pressure mounts. Worse yet, they suddenly realize they are following a man who is totally opposed by everybody with any authority. Their leader is seen as a curse by leaders of society. Because they are associated with him, they are cursed as well. They continue in this process of following until they are headed for a crash.

The disciples have followed Jesus and he has given them the simple model of "I'll do, you watch." Then he begins saying, "I'll do, but you help." He sends them out to do things he has been doing: preach the gospel, heal the sick, cast out demons. He sends out the Twelve (Luke 9:1–2) and tells them to feed more than five thousand people (Luke 9:10–17). The disciples quickly become overwhelmed and lose confidence.

Then we see two groups who had a deep hatred for each other, the Herodians and the Pharisees, come together in a common bond against Jesus and his followers (Luke 11:53). At this point the disciples fall into despair. Their early enthusiasm is gone; the reality of their decision to follow Jesus sets in. They lack confidence, experience, and enthusiasm. They are anxious and feel vulnerable to the opposition that has arisen in response to Jesus' teaching. They literally fear for their lives. Maybe it's time to lie low. Jesus isn't helping things. He stirs the pot by saying a lot of radical things about the Pharisees and Sadducees. The disciples are thinking, "Man, he's making them mad. They're going to kill us."

Amid the fears of the disciples, how does Jesus respond? He changes his directive style of leadership to more of a coaching style, appropriate to this new situation. Now he shares his vision and grace with the disciples. Now he looks for ways to spend more time with them. Now he starts giving explanations. He's pressing in on them so that they realize where they are. After he squeezes the sponge so that their false sense of enthusiasm is gone, he's ready to get down to business. And they're finally ready to listen. They begin going to faraway places just to get away from people. Jesus spends more time alone with his followers in order to relieve their fears and help them focus on what it means to live a kingdom life.

In Jesus' leadership style, experience comes before explanation. The disciples just had a near-death experience at the hands of the Pharisees. Jesus comes in behind this experience with an explanation of why they do not need to fear these events.

Do not be afraid, little flock, for the Father has been pleased to give you the kingdom. Sell your possessions and give to the poor. Provide purses for yourselves that will not wear out, a treasure in heaven that will not be exhausted, where no thief comes near and no moth destroys. For where your treasure is, there your heart will be also.

—Luke 12:32–34

In essence, Jesus is telling the disciples to let go of their old securities. He wants them to find their security in him. Until this point, the disciples probably thought they were going to flamboyantly usher in this magnificent kingdom of God. Now they are unsure that anyone can bring it in, and they certainly don't think it will be them. They're scared. Jesus reminds them about grace. It's not what they can do for God, it's what God can do through them. They needed to understand that the kingdom of God is given, not earned; received, not taken. They could not do the work of the kingdom themselves. The kingdom comes only by grace, not works. They began to learn and believe this.

Stage 2 is when the excitement begins to die down and the feelings of incompetence and inexperience come to the forefront. Disappointments pile up; expectations are not fulfilled. Opposition and difficulty become overwhelming. The disciple forgets the vision and begins to question how well he or she really understood it to begin with. There are no highs to balance the lows.

> The kingdom comes only by grace, not works.

Disciples realize they are ill-equipped for the what they set out to do and soon are in the deep pit of despair.

Get the picture?

Disciples are flailing around trying to figure out what to do. They tend to try to regain the enthusiasm of Stage 1. Many of us go back and forth between Stage 1 and Stage 2 again and again. Instead of allowing God to take us completely through our vulnerability in Stage 2, we want to ignore it and go back to the feelings we had in Stage 1. But soon we crash back into Stage 2 again. If we do not have a leader to take us *through* Stage 2, we will bounce back and forth between enthusiasm and despair, with the two coming at ever-closer intervals. We must receive the grace that comes only by going all the way through the uncomfortable phase.

Stage 2 is the most important in the development process for a disciple. The child on the bicycle begins to think maybe it's not so cool to learn to ride after all. He's had a happy life until now without a two-wheeler; why does he need one now? Do you give up on teaching this child to ride? Of course not. You repeat your instructions, and this time you know the child will take them seriously. The earlier naïve enthusiasm is transformed into attentiveness to you.

The leadership style that meets the needs of this stage is a coaching style. This leader gives direction and demonstrations, but now the leader invites discussion. Is the disciple really understanding? Does the disciple feel free to ask questions based on some experience? The leader is more available to the disciple on a personal level.

Leaders need to be there to offer God's grace and encouragement on a personal, individual level. While the disciple is bouncing around between Stage 1 enthusiasm and Stage 2 despair, the leader can offer a ladder to get out of the pit. The two rungs on this ladder are grace and vision.

When a person is in a time of discouragement and despair, vision is

> When a person is in a time of discouragement and despair, vision is critical.

critical. When you don't know where you are going or what you are looking for, you need a vision. Painting a vision for others does not mean glossing over the hard truth. Whether it's riding a bike, playing football or living as a disciple, a vision simply allows the learner to say, "Okay—this is what I signed up for. It's harder than I thought, but I'm ready now. Let's go."

Stage 2 is the testing point of any leader, even if you're leading just one other person. During this stage, clear your schedule and spend time down in the pit with the individual or team going through Stage 2. If you're potty training, be ready to spend a lot of time in the bathroom with your toddler clapping enthusiastically at every sign of cooperation. If you're teaching geometry, be ready to draw the segments and shapes over and over, answer the questions over and over. If you're mentoring a disciple, be ready to answer questions and explain as much as necessary.

At this stage of discipleship we learn that we can continue on only by God's grace, not by our lifting ourselves up by our bootstraps. Grace is an incredibly difficult concept for us as humans to grasp. We all like to think we're in control and can look after ourselves. When we learn grace, we learn it's not up to us—we are simply following God's directions to accomplish his purpose. He will always accomplish what he wants done. It is amazing what happens when one person can take another out of fruitless striving and into a place of resting in grace. Confidence begins to grow because the person is seeing God's work by grace, not the results of human effort.

Once we stop bouncing back and forth between the highs of Stage 1 and the lows of Stage 2, we're ready to move forward.

FOR MORE ON PRINCIPLES OF GROWTH, SEE THE HEPTAGON, CHAPTER 20

Chapter 14

From Learners to Leaders

Jesus invested methodically in training his disciples so they could continue the work he had begun—calling people to be part of the kingdom of God. He made leaders out of a motley bunch of fishermen and tax collectors, and the world was never the same. We are leaders in order to lead others to Jesus. We have no greater goal in life than to make disciples.

Let's take a closer look at the stages of learning and leadership that take us past the times of discouragement and on to commitment.

Stage 3

Disciples have growing confidence.
Leaders are open to discussion.

Stage 3 disciples are starting to get the hang of things. Enthusiasm is back, but this time it is based on some real knowledge of what the task is. Confidence in their ability to accomplish the task may wax and wane, but generally a sense of competence moves in the upward direction. The rider is back on the bicycle, this time knowing there is a lot to learn. The child may be saying, "Don't let go! Don't let go!" but the fact is that he is pedaling faster and steering straighter with every yard, and soon you'll have no choice but to let go. It may be a while before the child realizes you're no longer there.

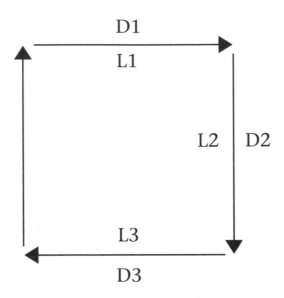

When he does, he squeals, "I'm doing it! I'm doing it!" Sticking with the challenge through Stage 2 has paid off.

Iyabo got a great new job. She loved it—it was the best job ever. After some time had passed, however, it started not being the best job ever. In fact, not a good job at all. It was time to move on and find another job. Perhaps the best job ever, a job she could really love. Or maybe not.

Iyabo enjoyed Stage 1 as a disciple, but Stage 2 was discouraging. Rather than finding her way through it, she would leave one job and seek to relive the feelings of Stage 1 by beginning a new job.

After a while she saw what she was doing. Once she understood the Square, she realized that the difficulties she experienced at Stage 2 were just that—a stage. She could work her way through this stage with her coworkers. Iyabo now knows that she can apply the principles of learning around the Square to any situation. She has started taking her friends through it—becoming the leader rather than the learner. She has set up a ministry to teenage girls in the inner city and uses the Square as a foundation for her ministry. Now as she works her way around the Square, she's in the Leader role.

The phrase that sets free a disciple experiencing Stage 2 is "God is in charge." At this point we have to acknowledge grace and begin to work it into our lifestyles. This is not easy for most of us, but it is the one thing that will move us on to growth and maturity. It is the one thing that will move us out of our childish ways that blow us in every wind of doctrine, that lead us to grasp at any new thing that comes along. Going to this conference, buying that new book, listening to a new tape, jumping around from church to church—all these can be substitutes for growing into the disciples God intends for us to be. We can get out of that trap and into a gradual growing process as the Lord works his grace into our hearts. As we live out the lessons learned in Stage 2, we once again grow in confidence and find that our enthusiasm increases.

At this stage the Twelve are spending a lot of time with Jesus. Strong friendship grows between the leader and the disciples. Jesus spends time with the Twelve to create an intimacy they had not previously felt with him. He calls them his friends at this stage. This is the kingdom in action.

What leadership style meets the needs of disciples in this stage?

Now is the time for consensus. The leader is less directive and welcomes discussion as a way to learn. The leader is available and accessible to followers for a personal relationship.

Jesus' increased time with the disciples begins to produce growing confidence. In this phase we see a period of growth in the disciples. This period of time is marked by less directive growth than the early stages of discipleship. Jesus did not begin his ministry by calling the disciples with this kind of message. They weren't ready for it. It would not have motivated them to follow Jesus. They needed to go through the pressures, discouragement, and threats until they reached their low point. Once there, they would cleave to Jesus and to one another.

Leadership has changed dramatically from a directive style to gathering consensus. Many leaders make the mistake of starting in this phase. In an effort to get "buy-in," they welcome all suggestions. They're trying to have a democratic style from the beginning. This simply will not work. The followers have to pass through Stages 1 and 2 before they have the experience and vision to offer credible opinions and suggestions. If you give decision-making ability to a disciple too soon, both the leader and the disciple will soon veer off course. The vision morphs into something that accommodates many different people, something that is not solid enough to move toward. Each phase must be allowed to run its full course.

Up until now, the disciples had been operating like hired hands, doing what they were told without really seeing the big picture. But now Jesus calls them his friends.

My command is this: Love each other as I have loved you. Greater love has no one than this, that he lay down his life for his friends. You are my friends if you do what I command. I no longer call you servants, because a servant does not know his master's business. Instead, I have called you friends, for everything that I learned from my Father I have made known to you.

—John 15:12-17

Friends have common objectives and share their lives together. At this point, relationships begin to get warm. They have communion together. They laugh more. Everything

> Friends have common objectives and share their lives together.

feels very different from Stage 1 and Stage 2. Now the disciples love to hang out together, share in the workload, linger after teaching sessions to discuss what they have heard and what it means. During this phase, Jesus has all the time in the world for them.

How wonderful this must have been for the disciples, hanging out at their upstairs barbeque, enjoying the wonderful feeling of listening to Jesus tell them they are his friends—his best friends. He loves them so much that he would lay down his life for them.

A lot of Christians get to this stage, especially in churches. "This is it! We're friends! We get to hug!" How much better could it get? There is more—just not necessarily better by human standards.

At this very comfortable stage of relationship with his disciples, Jesus drops a bombshell.

Jesus tells the disciples he will be leaving them soon. He says he is going to prepare a place for them in the Father's house, and that they know how to get to where he is going. The disciples are confused. "What's he talking about?" "Wait a minute; didn't you just say we were friends? Why are you leaving us?

The disciples start to flirt with the feelings of Stage 2 again. This may happen with those you lead. Thomas speaks for them all and says, "We don't know where you are going, so how could we know the way?" (John 14:5). Jesus answers with perhaps the defining statement of all of mankind's existence. "I am the way, the truth and the life" (John 14:6).

But the disciples still don't get it. They are happy where they are and don't want this wonderful time to end. All that pain and suffering in the beginning, and now this. The disciples thought they had already endured the hard times. We might even say they were over-confident. Why should anything change now?

Something like this may happen with disciples you are leading as you prepare to ease yourself out of leadership. But remember, the disciples have the vision; they know the direction they should be moving in.

Jesus was preparing his friends for the final phase of discipleship.

STAGE 4

Learners are confident and competent.
Leaders give low direction, low examples.

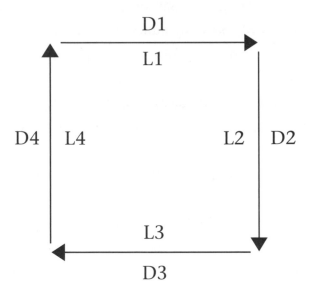

We are almost around the Square. In this "home stretch" the disciple has caught the vision and has practiced living it out. Enthusiasm is high and confidence is high because experience is high. All this adds up to a high level of competence to do the job without the leader. In other words, the disciple is ready to be a leader and start the square all over again with others as the disciples.

The high enthusiasm of this stage is not just froth and bubble. It has deep roots in confidence, brought about by a strong feeling of experience and competence. Stage 3 has brought growth and experience. Confidence that once was lost now has begun to return. The team now has competence. The leader takes into account what the team thinks and seeks to build consensus. The leader depends less on being an example because at this stage the disciples should be doing the work.

> Good leaders always get people to the stage where they are ready to accept delegated responsibility.

What kind of leadership does the disciple need now?

At this stage, the leader offers very little direction. Instead, the leader asks experienced learners what they think. Learners are ready to enter into the discussion, to contribute to planning and strategy.

It is now time to delegate authority and responsibility. Good leaders always get people to the stage where they are ready to accept delegated responsibility. Delegating to disciples before this stage is a recipe for disaster. They may think they are ready, but until they have been completely through the first three stages, they are not. As a leader, you may find yourself in a "You do, I fix" position. That does not create new leaders.

Leaders must always be looking to give away their jobs to people who can do them as well or better than they. The delegation process goes through four stages that correlate with the discipleship stages.

- Stage 1—"I do, you watch."
- Stage 2—"I do, you help."
- Stage 3—"You do, I help."
- Stage 4—"You do, I watch."

Continually hearing Jesus' teaching and putting it into practice sends roots down deep, strengthening the disciple against the inevitable storms. The disciple's confidence is in God. The disciple is ready to move on out.

Then Jesus came to them and said, "All authority in heaven and on earth has been given to me. Therefore go and make disciples of all nations, baptizing them in the name of the Father and of the Son and of the Holy Spirit, and teaching them to obey everything I have commanded you. And surely I am with you always, to the very end of the age."

—Matthew 28:18-20

Sure enough, Jesus is taken away from his disciples. He is arrested, tried, crucified. He comes back again, yes, but this time as the resurrected Lord. He doesn't hang around with the disciples all the time the way he did before. He just turns up every so often and in the most surprising ways. They have all the doors and windows locked and all of a sudden Jesus is there (John 20:19). They are afraid and at one point Jesus says, "Go and tell my brothers to go to Galilee; there they will see me" (Matt. 28:10). So they all go off to Galilee. They search and look, but no Jesus. Not knowing what to do next, they go back to the only other thing they know to do—they go fishing. In the morning, after a fruitless night of not catching fish, they see someone on the beach (John21:7). Guess who it is?

Jesus is preparing the disciples to spend less time with him. He is reducing their hours of contact with him because he is now delegating authority. He is giving them the job he had done; they are to become his representatives. In this last stage the disciples are empowered with confidence and competence as a result of their deeper relationship and ministry experience with Jesus.

We have seen the change in discipleship from the very first phase where Jesus says, "Come, follow me" to the last stage where he says, "Go out into all the world and do what I have taught you to do." As the stages of discipleship grow and change, Jesus adjusts his leadership accordingly. He has taken the disciples through a process of development to equip them for their new task—taking the Gospel into the world.

At this point, Jesus says, "Go and do what I have done—make disciples like I have."

CHAPTER 15

ALL YOU'RE MADE TO BE

*G*od does not expect you to be who you are not.

Does that bring you some relief?

God has buckets full of grace to pour out on us—but we have to be standing where the downpour is. When we walk the path God has called us to walk, we will discover grace beyond our expectations.

God does not expect you to be who you are not, but he does want you to be all that he made you to be. When we know what we have been designed for and called to do, we can save ourselves a lot of striving in areas we were not built for. If we know who God has made us to be, we can stop trying to be someone we are not and let go of the stress that comes with living that kind of life. God has made you to fit in a certain place where you can serve him best, where he can shower you with grace.

One of the ministry roles that we will discuss in the following chapter is that of Prophet, or one through whom God reveals inspired revelations. Well, think of a person who typically fulfills this prophetic role in his ministry and

> God does not expect you to be who you are not, but he does want you to be all that he made you to be.

makes a sudden attempt at teaching. He spends hours and hours preparing lessons, never feeling 100 percent certain that he is on the right track. Once the lessons begin, his students often seem confused, disorganized or lack a specific focus. No matter how hard he tries, the prophet turned teacher just can't seem to get things right in terms of instructing his class, and his frustration is mounting. How would this person fare as a senior pastor or even a small group leader? Would he do a good job? Would he even enjoy the work?

Discovering and acknowledging who God has made you to be will ensure you are standing under the bucket of grace, not beside it. So let's see how to figure out where you belong so you'll be under that shower of grace and get a healthy soaking, not just a splash.

A SPIRITUAL GIFT IS NOT YOUR MINISTRY

Several New Testament passages speak of gifts for the church, including 1 Corinthians 12, Romans 12, 1 Peter 4, and Ephesians 4. Most of us have learned that God has given us one or several of the gifts listed in these passages. You can go through any number of exercises and programs meant to help you find your spiritual gift. However, there is an important distinction between spiritual gifts and roles. A spiritual gift is not a ministry in itself. Rather, it is a tool to use for the job at hand. That job is the role or function you are called to. To help in differentiating the gifts from a specific role, let's look at the context of two of the New Testament churches that received these letters.

Both 1 Corinthians 12 and Romans 12 contain lists of gifts. Many Bible teachers take both lists, try to eliminate any overlap, and come up with a comprehensive list of spiritual gifts. They speculate about why the lists are not identical. They suggest that special abilities not on this list are "talents" rather than spiritual gifts.

What we often overlook is that Paul wrote these letters to different churches facing distinct problems. He wrote to each of these bodies, the churches at Corinth and Rome, to teach them about grace and how to apply it to their particular situations. Paul aimed his teaching at two different targets.

The Christian church in Corinth had questions about Christian conduct when the believers gathered for worship or fellowship. Paul had heard of some practices that disturbed him, and the church had written to him with specific questions. In 1 Corinthians, Paul devotes four chapters to instructions about public worship. He addresses problems arising from this particular church's gatherings.

> The dancing hand of the Holy Spirit causes us to exercise one or more of the gifts.

The church at Corinth struggled to understand corporate worship. As part of his instructions about worship, Paul writes about spiritual gifts.

In 1 Corinthians 12, Paul explains that believers should expect the Holy Spirit to be present in power when they gather. The key word to understanding how the Holy Spirit works is "manifestation" in verse 7. In Greek, the word is *phanerosis*, meaning the revelation or enlightening that God brings. The English word we use for this has its roots in the Latin for "the dancing hand." Isn't that great? The dancing hand of the Holy Spirit falls on certain individuals during a gathering, causing them to exercise one or more of the gifts—wisdom, words of knowledge, tongues, prophecy, and so on. Anyone can receive any of the manifestations, or the dancing hand, of the Spirit mentioned in 1 Corinthians 12.

Paul was saying that in corporate worship the Spirit will fall on certain individuals, giving them gifts for the moment. These are not permanent roles; we do not possess these gifts as our own "ministry." The key to the gifts is the Spirit moving as a dancing hand within our gathering, dispensing grace as it is needed.

Now let's sail on to Rome, where the church faced a different set of practical issues. The Book of Romans is quite theological, heavy on doctrinal teaching. Paul carefully explains God's faithfulness in bringing salvation to people who don't deserve it. And none of us deserves it. We're all sinners. We are all under a death sentence. But in Christ, God gives us the very righteousness we need. We are all justified by faith.

In Rome, Jews and Gentiles were not seeing everyone alike as Paul intended. Despite a common faith, the church struggled with ethnic division. They were not functioning as the single united church God meant for them to be.

In Romans 12, Paul tries to help the church in Rome get past the growing rivalry and division that existed between Jews and Gentiles. He pleads with them, in view of everything he has shown them about God's mercy and grace, to live sacrificial lives. He wants them to stop arguing and start living their lives for one another. Sacrifice and service are the context of this passage. Paul gives some practical examples: If your gift is teaching, stick to teaching. If it is to give aid to those in need, keep your eyes open for opportunities. This is not meant to be an exhaustive list of roles within the church, merely a few examples used to make a point.

Both Romans and 1 Corinthians were written to specific churches facing specific problems and circumstances. In contrast, the Book of Ephesians was not written to just one church for a special moment in time, but for the all the churches in the region of Asia Minor. Paul seems to have left off the personal greetings that pepper many of his letters because he knew this letter would be read widely around the region. It doesn't address specific problems, but rather outlines foundational teachings for how a church should function. Paul wrote to expand believers' understanding of God's purpose and their part in it. God has high goals for the church, and he works out these goals in the daily lives of believers. In Ephesians Paul shares what the roles of all believers are to be within the church as they serve God's purpose.

THE FIVEFOLD MINISTRIES ARE FOR EVERYONE

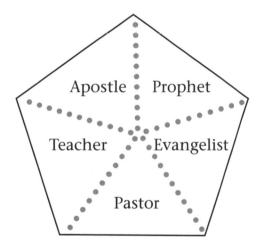

But to each one of us grace has been given as Christ apportioned it. . . It was he who gave some to be apostles, some to be prophets, some to be evangelists, and some to be pastors and teachers, to prepare God's people for works of service, so that the body of Christ may be built up until we all reach unity in the faith and in the knowledge of the Son of God and become mature, attaining to the whole measure of the fullness of Christ.

—Ephesians 4:7, 11–13

"But to each one of us . . ."

Traditional teaching says that the fivefold ministries in this passage are five roles for leaders in the church. But what about that phrase, "But to each one of us. . .?"

"To each one" refers to every member of the church, not just leaders. Each one of us has received a portion of grace in at least one of five roles. That grace has come to us in the form of a call to be one of five types of people. There is no mention of leadership in this passage. This is not just for those who have been ordained or have been through seminary. The fivefold ministries in Ephesians 4 are for you and for me, for "each one of us."

". . . grace has been given as Christ apportioned it."

The fivefold roles apply to all members of the body of Christ in varying degrees. Paul says that Jesus, by the gift of his grace, has empowered and equipped each of us for service. We have all been given different-sized portions of grace and anointing. We each receive part of the whole. Christ's ministry fully demonstrates all five roles of apostle, prophet, evangelist, pastor, and teacher. As members in his body, we receive at least one of these five appointments, relying on one another for those areas we are not gifted in.

"It was he who gave some to be apostles, some to be prophets, some to be evangelists, and some to be pastors and teachers, to prepare God's people for works of service so that the body of Christ may be built up."

These five gifts of grace seem to be the elements needed to prepare people for service and building up the church. Each person receives a portion of grace to fulfill a ministry role as an apostle, prophet, evangelist, pastor, or teacher.

"Until we all reach unity in the faith and in the knowledge of the Son of God and become mature, attaining to the whole measure of the fullness of Christ."

When each person is working, by grace, in the role given by the Holy Spirit, the result is unity in faith, a continual growing in the personal knowledge of Jesus, and maturity or wholeness, which all lead to the fullness of Christ.

When we look at each part of the passage in context, we see clearly that the gifts in Ephesians 4 are roles or functions given to each believer. The gifts mentioned in 1 Corinthians and Romans are tools to enable all believers to function more effectively in those roles.

When all the roles of apostle, prophet, evangelist, pastor, and teacher are operating effectively within a church, then all the people are being prepared for service and are being built up. The results will be unity, knowledge of Christ, spiritual maturity, and the fullness of Christ. What a great picture of how the church should look! How liberating to know that you do not have to do it all. None of us has to do it all. God has called everyone to take a part in his body. He will always accomplish what he wants done.

SERVING THE SERVANT KING

Our source for each LifeShape is Jesus. As we look at the five ministries of the Pentagon, we might ask, which one was Jesus' role? The answer, of course, is all of them. Jesus fulfilled all five roles in his ministry on earth. That means that he is our model no matter which ministry we are gifted in.

In each LifeShape, we are reminded that Jesus came as a servant. Servants do not serve by giving of their time, talents, or possessions. In Jesus' time, servants had nothing to give. Nothing. Servants must receive before they can give. Jesus told his disciples: "The Father loves the Son and has placed everything in his hands" (John 3:35). Jesus came into this world as a servant with nothing except what he received from the Father.

God does not expect you to be what you are not. But he does mean for you to be a servant minister, knowing that you have nothing to offer except what God himself gives you.

> You have nothing to offer except what God himself gives you.

Should we jostle and fight with one another to determine which ministry is the most important? Should we place ourselves above our fellow servant ministers? Of course not. As we consider each ministry, and you find your role, remember that we are following Jesus, the Servant King.

CHAPTER 16

GET ON BASE

*A*postle. Prophet. Evangelist. Pastor. Teacher. Those are heavy-duty words. Or are they?

It's not God's idea to weigh us down with these words. God's plan is to liberate us with these words. God made each of us to serve him, but we serve in different ways. We have to remember that God made us as whole people—we're not chopped up into how we are at home, how we are at work, how we are at church. Our personalities weave together all the aspects of our lives. The characteristics that make us who we are show up whether we're at the grocery store or a worship service. And God knows exactly how he wants to put our personalities to work. Ephesians 4 tells us about five areas of ministry. But despite the heavy-duty sounding words, we find our personalities generally reflected in these five areas. So let's look at each of them more carefully. Then you'll be able to examine your own base ministry and the phases of your service in God's kingdom.

> We're not chopped up into how we are at home, how we are at work, how we are at church.

I was a pastor who served the same church in the same community for more than 30 years. However, I believe I was anything but stuck. The community I lived in was just outside New York City, and the population constantly shifted as people were transferred in and out of jobs in the area. Although I stayed put, I recognized that I was "sent" to a new congregation about every five years. The challenges of my ministry changed as the mix of people in my congregation shifted.

—*PASTOR DAVID*

APOSTLE

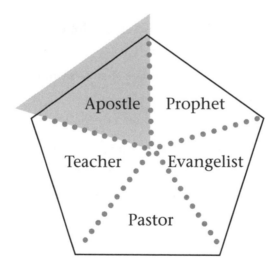

An apostle is one who is "sent out." Apostles are visionary and pioneering, always pushing into new territory. They like to establish new churches or ministries. They come up with new, innovative means to do kingdom work. They enjoy dreaming, performing new and challenging tasks. Change is always a good thing. The explorers of the great West in the United States were like this. And if Lewis and Clark had not taken their exploratory journey, what might the United States be like today? The names of people you know may be springing to mind right now—not because they pioneered the Wild West, but because they can't seem to sit still; they're constantly searching for some new interest to explore. Business entrepreneurs are another example of this kind of person—someone eager to conquer the next business frontier, only to move on to some new endeavor after that.

Jesus is the One sent by God (John 3:16). In turn, he prepared others to go on to the next kingdom frontier. The twelve disciples didn't huddle in Jerusalem for long. They spread out around the expanse of the Roman Empire. Paul encountered Jesus unexpectedly on the road to Damascus and became the Apostle to the Gentiles. Priscilla and Aquilla were believers in Rome who then pioneered new churches with Paul.

PROPHET

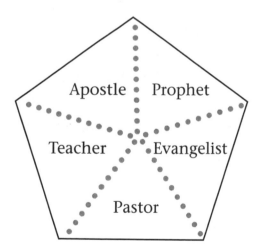

The prophet hears and listens to God. Sometimes the prophet is the one who can stand back from circumstances to get a clear picture of what is happening. This clarity of vision results in creative solutions and a vision

I was a college student involved in leading Bible studies and worship at my church. People around me really seemed to appreciate my ministry and they let me know that. I felt that I was good at what I was doing. But most of the time, I felt like a square peg in a round hole. I just didn't fit, something wasn't quite right.

Then I found myself discussing with a ministry team whether or not you can *hear* God. Can you know exactly what God is saying? At first I found the discussion a bit strange. But it wasn't long before I found myself in that position—I had encountered a situation and had a distinct sense of what was going to happen. And I was right. As I looked at people, particular verses from Scripture came to mind that were specifically applicable to those people. When a friend asked me to pray for him, I wrote down everything I felt God was saying to me about that situation. Later, everything I had written down happened. It was then that I realized that I may be good at teaching, but I have a strong prophetic gift. Indeed, I *hear* God.

—*ELISEO*

for situations that others don't see. Prophets understand the times and what people should do. They enjoy being alone with God, waiting, and listening. Prophet personalities in the world in general are often creative people—musicians, artists, people who speak out their perceptions.

Every word spoken from the mouth of Jesus was a revelation from God. He often foretold events, such as Peter's denial and the details of his own death. He himself is the fulfillment of Old Testament prophecy such as Isaiah 53, foretelling the coming of the Messiah.

In Luke 2, Anna and Simeon prophesied over the infant Jesus, recognizing him as the salvation that God provided for his people. In Acts 11:28, Agabus predicted a severe famine in the Roman world and later, in Acts 21:11, took Paul's belt and prophesied about Paul's imprisonment. Philip's daughters, mentioned in Acts 21:9, were all known as prophetesses.

Though my role is senior pastor, I'm an evangelist at heart. Learning the principles of the Pentagon has truly enlightened me. It was freeing to have the permission to operate as God made me, in my area of ministry. It's like the alignment of the wheels on your car—you go in the right direction.

—WALT

EVANGELIST

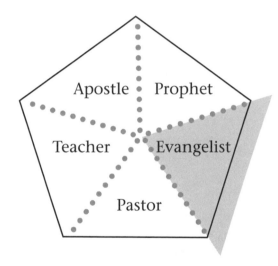

The evangelist brings the Good News and shares the message readily. Evangelists love spending time with non-Christians and often remind other Christians that non-Christians are still out there in the world. Evangelists are not necessarily all Billy Grahams, but they do tend to be "people gatherers." When they enter the room, others are drawn to them, and somehow they make each person feel like he or she is only person that matters. Salesmen, politicians, and public relations representatives are good secular examples of the personality type of evangelists.

Evangelists know the Word and can make it relevant to non-Christians. They enjoy discussion and sharing their point of view. Wherever they go, they seem to draw others into discussion about Jesus. They are passionate about sharing the Gospel. They are not timid about their faith and seem to easily share it with others regularly. Maybe you know some people like this.

Jesus embodied the Good News. He *was* the Good News. His encounter with the Samaritan woman at the well in John 4 is a good example of Jesus the evangelist in action. He dared to cross cultural boundaries and speak to someone the world disdained.

In Acts 8:12, the people believed Philip when he preached the Good News of the kingdom of God.

PASTOR

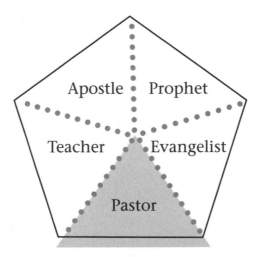

A pastor cares for others with a tender heart. The pastor sees needs, provides comfort and encourages others. Pastors spend most of their time with

---

For a long time, I didn't realize what my base ministry was. I thought I might be a Pastor, because I was always keenly aware of the needs of others around me and was moved to do something to meet those needs. But I wasn't very touchy-feely and was uncomfortable being a shoulder for someone else to lean on. "Can you have a pastoral ministry if you don't like people?" I wondered. I came to understand that I expressed my compassion by setting up systems to support larger numbers of people rather than ministering one to one. Because of my involvement in these areas I scored high as a Pastor on the Fivefold Ministry Questionnaire.*

—LOUISE

---

other Christians. They can easily empathize with others and exhibit lots of patience with those in need. Counselors, social workers, nurses and others in care-giving professions give us examples from life at large. Or you may have a friend who is not in any of these professions but is someone many people find easy to talk to. Pastors enjoy one-on-one chats and showing hospitality. They feel the burden of others' problems and have a knack for speaking the truth in love. They are good listeners and are easy to talk to and share inner feelings with.

Jesus refers to himself as the Good Shepherd who has come to care for his people (John 10). The shepherd knows the name of each sheep and loves them all enough to give his life for them.

In Acts 15:36–40, Barnabas demonstrates a pastoral heart. He was traveling with Paul and wanted to go back and see how the people were in towns they had already visited. He also wanted to give John Mark a second chance, after Mark had lapsed in his work with Paul and Barnabas.

---

* YOU CAN TAKE THE FIVEFOLD MINISTRIES QUESTIONNAIRE IN *A PASSIONATE LIFE WORKBOOK*. VISIT WWW.LIFESHAPES.COM FOR MORE INFORMATION

When I first took the Fivefold Ministries Questionnaire, I hated the fact that I
came out as a Teacher. I had just completed my first year of teaching in school
and it had been a very hard, very painful time. Members of the staff had told me
maybe this was not the career path for me and I had lost all confidence. But when I
learned from LifeShapes that a teacher is someone who reveals the Truth to others, I
began to see things differently. I discovered that a teacher has a broader role than
just giving information—it involved mentoring, discipleship. I began mentoring
younger women in our church and loved it! But one of my greatest experiences has
been teaching the LifeShapes course. I love being involved in opening people's eyes
to truths they have not seen before.

—JANELLE

TEACHER

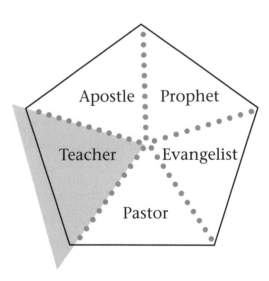

The teacher holds forth the Truth and is excited by it. Teachers look for
ways to explain, enlighten, and apply truth. They enjoy reading and study-

ing the Bible and helping others to understand it. In life at large, we see this kind of person in lecturers, teachers, and trainers of various sorts.

Jesus was often referred to as Teacher or Rabbi. His "students" often remarked that his teaching was different because he taught with authority.

In Acts 18, Priscilla and Aquilla plied their tent making trade with Paul in Corinth after Jews were banned from Rome. They traveled on with Paul to Ephesus. After Paul left Ephesus, a man named Apollos turned up. He taught with great enthusiasm but didn't quite have all the facts. Priscilla and Aquilla invited him to their home and explained the way of God to him. Apollos went on to have a fruitful teaching ministry.

BASE AND PHASE MINISTRIES

Each of us has a base ministry that represents one of the fivefold ministries in Ephesians. This ministry is from God and is for life. Hence we call this our "base ministry."

> We all have a base ministry and at least one phase ministry at any given time.

Alongside this are particular periods of time when God leads us to discover and understand the other ministries for a brief time. This is what we call our "phase ministry." We all have a base ministry and at least one phase ministry at any given time.

For example, the Lord may call you to go on a short-term mission trip (evangelist) or teach a Bible course (teacher), but these may not necessarily be the ministries that you feel most comfortable with. The Lord may give you a vision and grace for initiating a new ministry within your church that requires you to be more apostolic. Your base ministry, however, is as a teacher. You are invigorated by the new challenge and stretched as you trust the Lord to see you through, but eventually the stress of operating outside of your base causes you to want to return to the area you really love and are energized by.

Your base ministry will be the one that refreshes you, the one you are most passionate about. The Lord, however, will mature you by taking you through each of the other ministries in phases. As you experience phases of ministries in other areas, your base ministry becomes richer and well rounded.

Remember Louise? After several years, she completed the fivefold ministry questionnaire again. This time she came out as "apostle." The change reflected her experience of leading a small group for two years and being in a position to express the need to develop new ideas. The questionnaire changes as you gain life and ministry experience. If you want to discover your ministry, you can't beat trying leadership. When you have the opportunity to express yourself, you find out exactly how you're made. But you also have to try your hand at other things you don't naturally enjoy. Then you'll know how much grace those things require!

A WARNING

It is easy to fall into the trap of feeling as though you need to excel in all five ministries all the time. But this only leads to burnout and a failure to focus properly on your base ministry. Worse still, you will not be making room for others around you to explore their base ministries.

How do you know the grace for your phase ministry has been used up and it's time to return to your base? Generally energy and enthusiasm dry up. You see less blessing and less fruit from your efforts, even though you are working with the same intensity. Eventually you experience less peace about what you are doing. Your thoughts turn back to doing what you really love and what comes naturally for you. Going back to your base ministry is the only thing that gives you a sense of peace.

We are not all called to be pastors, be we are all called to care.

We are not all called to be teachers, but we are all called to hold out the Truth.

We are all responsible for learning how to listen for God's voice, something that comes more naturally for the prophet. We are all called to share the Good News with others, but this takes all those who are not called to be evangelists out of their comfort zones.

And we are not all apostles, but must all learn to walk out into what God calls us to do, however uncomfortable we are.

We are the body of Christ, which means that together, we represent the ministry of Jesus who was the embodiment of all five ministries in Ephesians 4. He is the perfect presentation of the ministry of the Spirit. By experiencing all five areas of ministry, whether as a base or a phase, we grow more into the likeness and character of our Master.

CHAPTER 17

FINDING—AND TAMING—THE FRONTIER

*N*ow that you see how every member of the body is equipped with one of the fivefold ministries as a base, you may be asking, "How do I know what my base gift is?"

One of the best ways you can begin to discover your base ministry is to take a look at your own personality—a true, honest look. Are you an introvert or an extrovert? This has nothing to do with how confident you feel. Being an introvert does not equal a lack of confidence. And not all extroverts feel confident all the time, even though they may appear so on the outside. Being an introvert or extrovert has to do with the way you function and process information. It can also give a clue as to your base ministry gift.

Extroverts often think by talking things through with others. Being in the company of others and participating in group activities refreshes an extrovert. The extrovert tends to work well with things that are immediate and can be seen quickly. Extroverts can speak confidently off the cuff. Many apostles, prophets, and evangelists tend to be extroverted.

Introverts think by internally processing things. An introvert is refreshed and recharged by reflection and spending time alone. Introverts are usually creative. Some of history's great writers, painters, and composers have been introverts. Introverted preachers feel much more comfortable when they have their entire sermon written out and displayed in front of them. Pastors and teachers tend to be introverted.

Of course this is not a clear-cut way to define one's ministry. Many people fall in the middle of the continuum between introvert and extrovert. Another measuring device for determining one's base ministry is to ascertain if one is a pioneer or a settler.

BLAZING THE TRAIL

The United States was expanded by the great efforts of pioneers and settlers. It was the pioneers who set out to map the land beyond the original American colonies. They met people who looked, lived, and spoke differently from them. Pioneers ate strange foods, learned new languages and discovered new routes to travel. They did not have maps to follow—they were the ones making the maps. Pioneers established towns and cities for the settlers that would follow.

Settlers were no less hardy than pioneers; they too had hardships to overcome. Getting a wagonload of household goods across the Rocky Mountains was no piece of cake. Pioneers may have built a town from stone and wood, but it was the settlers who established laws to keep that town safe. Settlers built schools to educate future generations. Settlers persevered through horrific weather and turned open prairie into the fruitful farmland. Someone who was injured or became sick went to a hospital that settlers built, and was cared for by doctors and nurses who had settled in that town to help and serve.

Both pioneers and settlers are necessary in the kingdom of God. Each acts differently in the approach to ministry roles. Pioneers, for example, enjoy change and find the stress of doing new things exciting rather than threatening. They love the challenge of making a breakthrough, trying something they haven't done before—insta-bility does not frighten them. In fact, it excites them. Whatever happens, they can make something of it, learn from it, turn

Both pioneers and settlers are necessary in the kingdom of God.

it into an adventure. They reach out beyond their current experiences and relationships to discover new frontiers and challenges. They are always look-ing for the next frontier to explore and tame. However, pioneers often find themselves bored and frustrated by the discipline necessary to sustain what they have established.

Settlers are a different breed altogether. They are committed to continuity, stability, and conservation. They're in it for the long haul, look-ing for long-term results. They prefer to grow and develop plans rather than scrap what they have and start over with something brand new. They are great at implementation. They like to see things through to the end. Settlers are the steady, solid backbone of most communities. They like to know what to expect and they feel most comfortable when things are moving smoothly according to plan. Instability causes great discomfort for settlers.

Pioneers and settlers do not always exist well together. The pioneer may get bored and restless if asked to stick around to help paint and decorate the buildings once they are up, and the settler can become uneasy at the thought of venturing into the wilderness of a new outreach ministry without the security of knowing what will happen. The pioneer says, "Come on, bring it on, let me run with the ball and see what happens." The settler says, "Slow down, we just want to focus on this right now."

Both pioneers and settlers, however, are vital elements to the service Christ has called us to. Without the pioneers we will never find the next

In my teenage years, I was planning to be an engineer. At the last minute before entering college, I decided to study dentistry instead, because it would combine science and working with people. Later I joined the Navy. I reveled in the travel and diversity and constant change that came with being in the Navy. After I got married, I felt that I should settle down—no easy task for someone like me. But I did settle down. I joined a church and became involved in pastoral activities, worship and working with college students. At the same time, I expanded my dentistry practice, adding staff and the newest equipment, looking for new and better ways to fix teeth. Despite what many people tend to think about the personalities of dentists, I was an entrepreneur.

When I learned about the Pentagon, a light bulb went on. Suddenly, I understood why I was the way I was, why I liked new things and different experiences. As I looked at my whole life—not just my work in the church—I saw that God had placed me in situations where I could launch new strategies, get things up and running, and then move on to the next challenge. I am a pioneer.

—NIGEL

frontier. We will not reach beyond what we have already achieved. Without the settlers, we would never sustain the frontier that the pioneers won. The pioneers will have pushed on to new territory, leaving the recently-discovered land barren. Settlers must come to build and occupy, to maintain and to increase through steady, deliberate efforts.

Pioneers look ahead to the frontier and seek to break new ground by putting visionary ideas into practice. Settlers consolidate the frontier the pioneer has won and play an important role in the continued health of the land.

The kingdom of God needs both pioneers and settlers, yet we must understand and appreciate the difference between the two. Otherwise division will swallow us up.

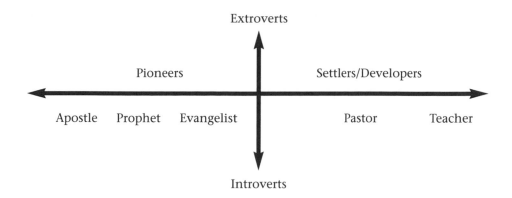

Pioneers naturally want to move into new methods and ideas to advance the kingdom. They are willing to take risks to join the Lord in new endeavors, often long before the settler even knows the Lord is moving in that direction. Off goes the pioneer, with an excitement that cannot be contained. This however can sometimes confuse the settler, who is working to preserve what has been handed down by previous generations. "It worked for them, so it will

> Mutual respect and acceptance for both pioneers and settlers are essential if kingdom work is to grow.

work for us" is the life motto of the settler. Settlers look to put down roots while pioneers are hacking through dense jungle growth in the search for new territory.

This is often why many churches split. It is not because of theology, but because members don't understand the interplay between pioneers and settlers. In some churches, the pioneers are driven away by settlers who do not want to explore anything new. In others, pioneers may cause division if they are not patient enough to wait for settlers to catch up with them.

Mutual respect and acceptance for both pioneers and settlers are essential if kingdom work is to grow.

OUT OF THE COMFORT ZONE

Of course, none of this is black and white. A person with a base ministry of teaching may be a pioneer with groundbreaking insights. A person with an apostolic base may be "sent" to the same work for many years. Each person falls at a point on the continuum between the two extremes, and can even move back and forth between the two. Different situations and circumstances draw us up and down the line. Those who handle stress and pressure the best are those who move most freely over the greatest distance on the pioneer/settler continuum.

> Testing comes into our lives to make us more flexible, to move us out of our comfort zones.

Testing comes into our lives to make us more flexible, to move us out of our comfort zones. God moves us by taking us into the territory we do not naturally feel comfortable in. You may recognize yourself as a pastor who feels sensitive toward the needs of other people. You want to help but your role also involves teaching other people how to care. Your base ministry will overlap other areas of ministry and this is how God challenges you.

When we move in a direction that is contrary to our natural instincts (a pioneer acting as a settler, for instance), we grow toward maturity. We do not grow by staying in our comfort zones. Once this period of testing is over, we then find relief by falling back on our strongest area of gifting, our base ministry. But if we never move into a phase ministry when God calls upon us, there will be no growth.

So how do you know what your base ministry is? Ponder what you know about yourself and your own ministry. In the end only God can confirm a calling. He has made each of us individually, with passions and desires that are unique to each one.

CHAPTER 18

SIX SIMPLE PHRASES

How many books on prayer do you own? How many have you seen on the shelves of Christian bookstores and thought you ought to own them? While we would all agree that God wants us to pray, and that we ourselves want to pray, still it remains difficult for many of us.

Almost every book on prayer seems to have been written by an introvert! I (Mike) am an extrovert. These books say something like, "To have an effective prayer life, it's important to spend four hours alone."

I stammer and stutter and say, "What was that word after hours? *Alone?* And do what?"

And the answer comes back, "Write in your prayer journal."

"A journal? Sit still and write? What for?"

That's not the kind of thing an extrovert does. Now suppose I hear an extrovert intercessor say something like, "Go for a walk. Look at the trees."

I think, "Okay, I can do that!"

"And involve God in your conversations."

"Yes! I can do that!" Prayer is something we should all feel we can do and do enthusiastically.

The twelve disciples were full-time students of Jesus, the Teacher. They learned practical faith by watching Jesus in action. Jesus spent a lot of time in prayer. The disciples could not help but notice. There was something about the way their teacher went about prayer that was different and caused them to want to pray the same way.

So the disciples come to Jesus and say, "Lord, teach us to pray." Perhaps they are expecting a long, complicated set of lessons and practice exercises. Jesus' answer was really quite simple—six phrases, with the instruction to "Pray like this."

Jesus only taught one method of prayer. We call it the Lord's Prayer, and we find it in Matthew 6 and Luke 11. If someone were to say to you "Pray like this," you could say, "Well, I'll consider your thoughts, but I'm sure there are many other ways to do it that I should probably also consider." But when *Jesus* says "Pray like this," we need to pay attention and do just as he says.

> Jesus only taught one method of prayer.

God is most interested in relationship—an open, ongoing relationship that we see throughout Scripture described as "walking with God." Life is learning to walk with God, learning to relate and communicate with God. How we interact with God is vital for our lives. Thus, when Jesus teaches his followers how to pray, he is showing them how to walk with God. If walking with God is truly what our lives are all about, then praying the way Jesus shows us is a major part of our life.

The Hexagon teaches us about prayer. The prayer Jesus taught has six elements. When we learn to pray these segments in the right way, we also learn to align our lives with God's will for us.

This, then, is how you should pray:
Our Father in heaven,
hallowed be your name,
your kingdom come,
your will be done
on earth as it is in heaven.
Give us this today our daily bread.
Forgive us our debts,
as we also have forgiven our debtors.
And lead us not into temptation,
but deliver us from the evil one.

—Matthew 6:9–13

THE FATHER'S CHARACTER

"Our Father in heaven, hallowed be your name."

Jesus begins with the simple word: "Father." The Aramaic word he used, *Abba*, is an informal name we often translate as "Daddy." Jesus used an intimate word for our intimate God. This was a shock to the disciples who were used to formal salutations in addressing God. They were no longer addressing a deity who was "up there somewhere," but a father, a dad. Jesus starts the whole prayer off by taking us straight into the court of the high king and telling us this is our dad. And we can talk directly with him.

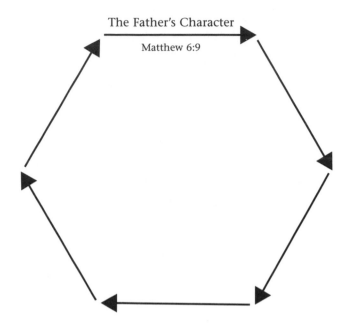

The Father's Character

Matthew 6:9

Most of us would have trouble starting our prayer with "Daddy." Funny, isn't it? God is showing us, through Jesus' prayer, that he loves us and wants for us to love him, yet we are the ones putting up walls. Try starting your prayer time with the intimate "Daddy" for a while and see what difference it makes as you talk with and listen to our Father.

Our father is "in heaven." We know right away we are talking with one who is near us but is separate from us. God is very close and yet is very different. He is the great "I AM," the mighty God, the Everlasting Father. There is none other like him; no other being approaches his greatness. Not only is he in heaven, he owns heaven. He made it. It is his realm, and we are invited into this holy place to speak one-on-one with its ruler.

Jesus goes on to remind us of the glory of God: "hallowed be your name." God's primary purpose for us is to glorify God and enjoy him forever:

Bring my sons from afar, and my daughters from the ends of the earth—every-one who is called by my name, whom I created for my glory, whom I formed and made.

—Isaiah 43:6-7

Glorifying God was the very reason Jesus gave himself in sacrifice:

It was for this very reason I came to this hour. Father, glorify your name!

—John 12: 27-28

When we pray "hallowed be your name," we recognize that God's chief purpose is to be hallowed, or glorified, in all that we do. We are aligning ourselves with the will of God our father.

THE FATHER'S KINGDOM

"Your kingdom come, your will be done."

Are you ready to enter the father's kingdom? Jesus says, "God has adopted you into his family. He wants to teach you who your father is." And the first thing we must know about our Daddy is that he is the king. Not only have we been adopted by a loving, wonderful father—and we can call him Dad—but he is the king. Not *a* king, *the* king. When you know who God is, you

> When you know who God is, you can say, "I want what you want, Daddy."

can say, "I want what you want, Daddy." God's kingdom is an awesome kingdom of light and love, and we want his kingdom to advance in this world of darkness and hate. Our desire is the same as the king's desire: to see everyone come out of this world of sin and into God's kingdom of forgiveness. We pray, "What you've done in heaven to remove sin and sickness and sadness and suffering and all that other stuff—let that be seen here on earth." After all, that's what Jesus means when he says, "The kingdom of God is at hand." The future we anticipate is breaking into the here-and-now. When we pray this phrase, we're praying for the future to break into the present so everyone can see it.

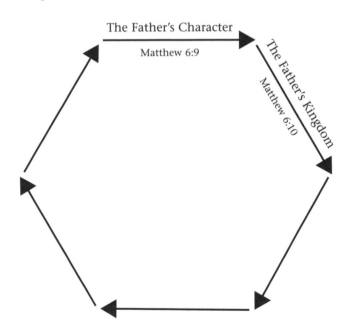

The Father's Character

Matthew 6:9

The Father's Kingdom

Matthew 6:10

When we say "kingdom," we can also say "kingship." The words here are one and the same. A king's kingship is his will—the way he will rule and reign in his kingdom. God's kingship—his will—is the very nature of God. As we pray this part of the Lord's Prayer, we are inviting the king to come

After I read this chapter on prayer I felt I understood a lot better how to pray . Imagine calling God, "Daddy." I asked my mom where all this information came from and she said "The Bible." "Then why," I asked, "hasn't anyone taught me this before?" This is really good stuff!

— MEGAN (AGE 14)

and rule in our lives. In times past when warfare was fought with swords instead of laser-guided bombs, when one man was captured by another, the prisoner would take his sword by the blade and extend the hilt toward his captor, thus signifying his surrender. "Your kingdom come, your will be done" is our surrender to the king.

THE FATHER'S PROVISION

"Give us today our daily bread."

The father's provision is abundant. We say, "Father, you are the king. I have needs. I depend on you. I sit at your table and take of all you have for me. I ask that everything I need for life you will provide, whatever that is. You are not lacking in anything, so I know I can come to you for everything I need in this life."

We humans are needy beings. We have needs in every area of our lives; food is just one of them. We have other physical needs that must be met daily—shelter, clothing, money to pay for all of this, employment to earn the money. We need health in our bodies. We need strength in our spirits. All of this is included in "our daily bread."

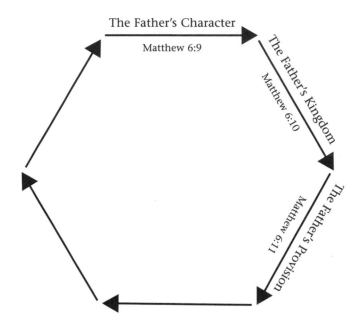

The Father's Character

Matthew 6:9

The Father's Kingdom

Matthew 6:10

The Father's Provision

Matthew 6:11

Notice that we are not told to pray for everything we will need for the rest of our lives, but only for today. So we are compelled to return to him over and over again. God delights in giving us what we need—and we need everything. As servants, we are empty-handed. But most of all God desires our attention and affection. If he were to give us the key to a vast bank vault and say, "Here is everything you will need throughout your life," how often would we be going back to him? Needs drive us to our knees. The children of Israel, wandering in the wilderness, were given manna for each day. If they took too much, the excess rotted and became maggoty before they could eat it the next day. If they forgot to gather the manna in the

> We are not told to pray for everything we will need for the rest of our lives, but only for today.

morning, they had to wait until the next day for more. Our bread from God is daily.

> Two things I ask of you, O LORD;
>> do not refuse me before I die:
> Keep falsehood and lies far from me;
>> give me neither poverty nor riches,
>> but give me only my daily bread.
> Otherwise, I may have too much and disown you
>> and say, "Who is the LORD?"
> Or I may become poor and steal,
>> and so dishonor the name of my God.

—Proverbs 30:7–9

THE FATHER'S FORGIVENESS

"Forgive us our debts, as we also have forgiven our debtors."

Jesus goes on to talk about sin. He says, "You know, there are boundaries to right behavior, and you're going to trespass those boundaries from time to time and find yourself in someone else's territory."

God has given us territory that is ours, and his provision within that territory is full and complete. Yet for some reason we stray from our land and try to take what is not ours. We trespass into our neighbor's land. All that we have in our lives has been given to us by God. When we transgress against another we are saying, "God, what you have given to me is not enough." And for this we must ask forgiveness. God has set a path for us; he has called us and given us a destiny. In this prayer we ask God to help us not to stray from his place for us within his kingdom, and to forgive us when we do.

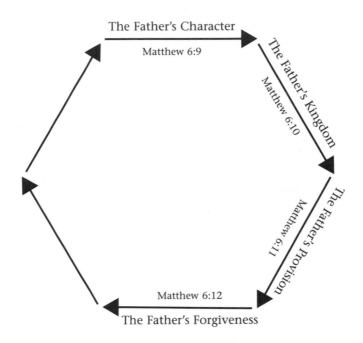

The Father's Character
Matthew 6:9
The Father's Kingdom
Matthew 6:10
The Father's Provision
Matthew 6:11
Matthew 6:12
The Father's Forgiveness

When other people stray from their paths onto ours, hurting us and abusing us and causing us pain, then we need to forgive them as God has forgiven us. "Keep us, Lord, from being indebted to you in withholding forgiveness from others." The father's forgiveness is never ending, but it is conditional, based on our willingness to forgive others.

THE FATHER'S GUIDANCE

"Lead us not into temptation."

Up until now, the prayer has dealt with our relationship with the Father and with those around us. ▲ The prayer changes, now dealing with our going out into the world with the message of God's love and forgiveness. "When you take us out into the world, Father, to do your bidding, to advance your kingdom, be sure to help us not to fall into the trap of the enemy." We have an enemy to our souls, and his devices of evil include temptation to participate in his evil. If we are led astray by his temptations, eventually we will end up in his hands. God promises to guide us around temptation so we are not ensnared. The trials and temptations in our world are not like a battle, they *are* a battle, one that we must fight every day. So be prepared for it and talk to your Father about the battle strategy.

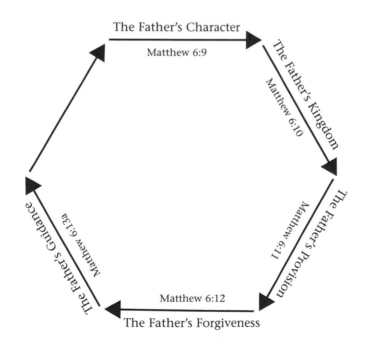

The Father's Character
Matthew 6:9

The Father's Kingdom
Matthew 6:10

The Father's Provision
Matthew 6:11

Matthew 6:12
The Father's Forgiveness

The Father's Guidance
Matthew 6:13a

▲ FOR MORE ON UP AND IN RELATIONSHIPS, SEE THE TRIANGLE, CHAPTERS 9 AND 10

THE FATHER'S PROTECTION

"And deliver us from the evil one."

The prayer ends, as it begins, by calling on God to intervene in our experience, pushing back the kingdom of darkness and extending the kingdom of heaven. The father's protection keeps us from the principalities and powers that seek to destroy us. The evil one comes only to steal and to kill, says Jesus. He wants to steal our health, steal our joy, steal our souls. If he is successful in his endeavors, we will enter into an eternal death in which we will forever be separated from the love of Christ. We are praying that God would protect us as we venture through life doing his will.

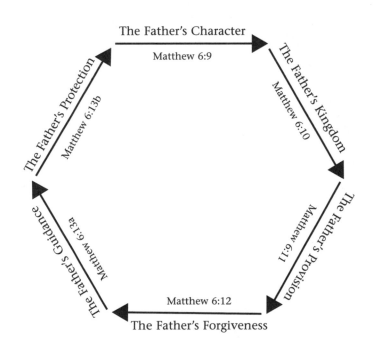

This prayer is a framework in which to pour all of the thoughts and concerns of your life. Take the thing most burning in your heart at the moment and pray through it using the prayer Jesus teaches us as the model. In this way you are communicating with God as he has taught us to. It really is that simple.

CHAPTER 19

THE LORD'S PRAYER FOR REAL LIFE

When we say Jesus only gave us one model of prayer, we do not mean to say that we pray these exact words and no more. When we say this model is simple, we do not mean that it is shallow. We must have a growing understanding of the six aspects of this prayer. We cannot remain static in our grasp of how Jesus taught us to pray—where there is no movement, there is no life. ● And too many Christians have lifeless times of prayer, led by those who have remained in the shallow end of the pool.

If Jesus said to pray in this way, did he do the same? In other words, did Jesus follow the model of the Lord's Prayer at other times when he prayed?

We have only short snippets of Jesus' other prayers recorded in the Gospels. He gives thanks before distributing bread and fish to a large group. He cries out in agony to his father in the garden before his arrest. And he cries to God while on the cross.

The only extended prayer of Jesus' that Scripture records is in John 17. Many call this the "true Lord's Prayer," because Jesus was praying for himself. In it, he models what he taught the disciples.

● FOR MORE ON MOVEMENT, SEE THE HEPTAGON, CHAPTER 20

- **The Father's character:** "Now this is eternal life: That they may know you, the one true God" (John 17:3).
- **The Father's kingdom:** "Father, glorify me in your presence with the glory I had with you before the world began" (vs. 5).
- **The Father's provision:** "Now they know that everything you have given me comes from you" (vs. 7).
- **The Father's forgiveness:** "I have brought you glory on earth by completing the work [mankind's salvation] you gave me to do" (vs. 4).
- **The Father's guidance:** "Sanctify them by the truth; your word is truth" (vs. 17).
- **The Father's protection:** "My prayer is not that you take them out of the world but that you protect them from the evil one" (vs. 15).

Jesus followed this model of prayer. Remember, we can't improve upon Jesus. Let's see how we can put the model Jesus gave us into practice in some specific ways.

STICKING POINTS

As you pray through this prayer, watch and wait—anticipate that God wants to speak to you through one of these areas. Picture the prayer as a bottle. You can use the bottle imagery for prayer in two ways. The first is to take your requests and drop them into the bottle. Pray through this model prayer with your request in mind, and see where it sticks. For instance, you can pray for your day:

> Pray through this model prayer with your request in mind, and see where it sticks.

"Father, I know you are my caring, loving, heavenly Father. You rule over all and will watch over me today from your throne in heaven. Let your glory be seen in all I do today. I want your rule and will to be done in all of my thoughts and actions today. Please provide for all of my needs today—spiritual, physical, financial."

Suppose this is where it sticks: you begin to think about the drawer full of bills you need to pay, but you are not sure where the money is going to come from. You pause to spend your time in prayer seeking God for the "daily bread" to pay your debts. You realize that it is the area of your life that you and God need to walk through together today.

Tomorrow the stopping point might be for forgiveness or for help in times of temptation. Each day will have at least one place that sticks out and grabs you as you pour your prayer into the bottle.

Another way to use this pattern of prayer is to pour prayer out of the bottle over each request. If someone you know is sick and asks you to pray, you can pray like this:

"Father, your reign in heaven extends down to our residence here on earth. Let your glory be seen in the life of my friend. In your kingdom there is no sickness, no pain. Let your kingdom come in my friend's life and body today. Providing our daily bread and our daily provisions includes having a healthy body so we can do all of your will, so please give my friend a healthy body today. Forgive my friend, as he forgives others, knowing that unforgiveness in our spirits can cause our bodies to react as well. Let him not be tempted to turn from you, his Healer, in this time of need. And protect him from the principalities and powers that want to cause him harm."

As you continue practicing the prayer, it becomes much easier to invite the Holy Spirit to prompt you to "stick" on one area at a time, whether you are praying for yourself or someone else. For instance, as you pray through the Lord's Prayer, perhaps you will pray:

"I am really having a problem with so-and-so in my small group. He has stomped in my garden over and over again. He is out of his territory and into mine. Nevertheless, I forgive him, Lord, just as you forgive me when I stomp in someone else's garden."

Perhaps you will stop on "your kingdom come, your will be done" as you consider what is going on in our world. As you think of an atrocity done to people in another country, you say:

"Lord, this does not look like your kingdom. Hate, not love, is reigning there, and that is not right. Let your kingdom rule be seen right now in that situation, and let love—which I know is your will—be felt by those people."

A PHRASE APART

Take one phrase per day from the Lord's Prayer and focus on it for your prayer time. Spend one day just thinking about what calling the God of the universe "Father" really means. If he truly is your Father, what responsibilities does he have toward you? What responsibilities do you have in your relationship with him? What does it mean that he is in heaven?

If you pray for God's kingdom to come, what will you expect to happen?

How can you demonstrate God's kingdom on earth?

If you're trusting in the Father's provision for each day's bread, what do you need to let go of? What are you secretly hoarding because you don't really think God will give you what you need?

> Each of the six segments of this prayer is bottomless.

And so on. Each day, pray through one of the phrases. Use that phrase to pray for the needs in your life and in the lives of those around you. If you feel you have reached the bottom of that phrase, that there is no more for you to get out of it, dig some more. Each of the six segments of this prayer is bottomless.

Another way to understand the Lord's Prayer is to see it as a circular prayer; each phrase is fully developed by all of the others. Take one phrase, place a colon after it, and then continue with the other phrases. Ask, how is this part of the prayer fully articulated in the rest of the prayer? Here's an example.

"Your kingdom come, your will be done":

- "Give us today our daily bread." God's loving desire is to meet all of our needs. In his kingdom, there is no want.
- "Forgive us our debts." In God's kingdom, our sins are washed away, never to be revisited.
- "As we also have forgiven our debtors." As we walk in the grace of God's forgiveness, we will forgive others. Freely we have received; freely we give. This is a law of kingdom life.
- "Lead us not into temptation." It is God's will that we walk the path he has laid out for us. In his kingdom, we will be fulfilled by all he has for us, and will not turn aside for a lesser, temporary fix.

My department at work meets twice a week to pray for one another's personal and work-related needs. After reading Mike's teaching on how to apply the Lord's Prayer to our daily life, our supervisor suggested one morning that we each focus on a particular facet of that prayer during our time together. We sensed a difference right away. It can be so difficult to know at times what to pray for in certain situations—and so easy to flounder around trying to think of what to say next. But with the simple elements of the Lord's Prayer guiding us, we felt a sense of purpose and direction—a centering of our petitions upon God. What better way to learn how to pray than from the example Jesus set?

—HOLLY

- "Deliver us from the evil one." The kingdom of God is all light; in it, darkness disappears. Principalities and powers that haunt us have no power in God's kingdom.
- "Our Father in heaven." The kingdom is ruled by a king—and the king is our dad! We can feel right at home in the kingdom. We are not strangers, but sons and daughters. We belong in God's kingdom.

Now you've come full circle. Start with any phrase, put a colon on the end and keep reading the rest of the phrases. Consider how that segment is played out in your life in the light of the rest of the prayer.

PERSONALIZE IT

We've mentioned praying until the Holy Spirit stops you. Using this method, focus on where you are stopped, and use your "sticking point" as a starting point. Ask yourself, "To what extent have I chosen to act like God in this area?" If you focus on "daily bread," think about how you are taking

God's place and are striving to meet your own needs. Then look left and right, as it were, at the other phrases. Look back to "hallowed be your name" and look ahead to "give us today our daily bread." How are you supplanting God in these areas? How are you trying to do God's work instead of trusting him to do it for you? This can lead to a time of repentance, cleansing us from the toxins that build up in us when we assume God's role.

Do you have a cell phone or a watch with an alarm that you can set? I (Mike) program my cell phone to give off a little beep six times throughout the day. Each time it reminds me to pause and pray one of the phrases of the Lord's Prayer. So at six in the morning, it's "Our Father in heaven." At nine, it's "Your kingdom come." At noon it's "Daily Bread." Toward the end of the working day it's "Forgive me," and later "Temptation." By the end of the day, it's a prayer for protection from evil.

When my phone beeps, no one thinks much about it—maybe it's a text message or a phone call I'll return later. If I feel really moved, I can leave a meeting for a couple of minutes and go out and pray the phrase

> Find your own trigger, your own reminder to pray.

without any real disruption to the group. This method is spreading as others realize how simple it is to give themselves reminders.

It doesn't have to be your phone. One man decided that whenever he saw a stop sign, he would pray one of the phrases of the Lord's Prayer. You can find your own trigger, your own reminder to pray.

FOR MORE ON THIS PRINCIPLE, SEE THE HEPTAGON, CHAPTER 21

Remember the triangle? Up, In and Out? If we look at the six phrases of the Lord's Prayer, we can easily see how they fall into couplets that remind us of the triangle.

UP

Our Father in heaven, hallowed be your name.

Your kingdom come, your will be done on earth as it is in heaven.

IN

Give us this day our daily bread.

Forgive us our debts, as we also have forgiven our debtors.

OUT

And lead us not into temptation.

But deliver us from the evil one.

These are just a few ways to explore these six short phrases Jesus gave us as a model for our prayers. As you can see, there is no end to how we can walk and talk with God using this model. As you begin using the principles of the Hexagon in your personal prayer life, you will no doubt uncover many other ways to apply this model. We believe you will see exciting changes in your prayer life.

CHAPTER 20

MEET MRS GREN

When you reached seventh grade, you learned (or should have learned!) that there are seven basic signs that a biological organism is alive. We'll bypass the pop quiz and just tell you what they are. (And you can say, "I knew that.") These seven functions of life are:

1. Movement
2. Respiration
3. Sensitivity
4. Growth
5. Reproduction
6. Excretion
7. Nutrition

Children in Great Britain commit these seven processes to memory using the acronym MRS GREN. And that is what we call the Heptagon in LifeShapes: MRS GREN, or life in the kingdom of God. Part of the discipleship process is looking at how our bodies—designed and built by God—operate in relation to our spiritual beings. The Heptagon deals with this biological-spiritual connection.

MOVEMENT

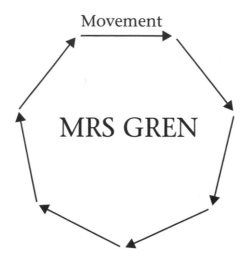

Movement

MRS GREN

On a cold day, 10-year-old Caleb loves to come in from the outside and put his frigid hands on the back of his mother's neck. She jumps every time.

A cougar may seem to be sleeping in the shade of a tree on a hot day—until it hears a noise in the bushes. Is it a bigger animal for whom the cougar would make a nice lunch? Or is it lunch for the cougar? Either way, the cougar now moves with amazing speed.

Caleb's mother and the cougar both responded to a stimulus with movement.

The children of Israel stand on the shores of the Red Sea. Behind them is Egypt and generations of slavery. Between them and a new land lies a body of water that is not exactly easy to cross. Besides, what happens when they get across? They don't know what they'll find. They hesitate.

Then word comes that Pharaoh's chariots are hot on their trail. The Israelites can't just stand there in hesitation. If they want to stay alive, they must move. At the perfect moment, God parts the waters of the Red Sea so two million people can walk across on dry land. How cool is that?

You'd think the people of Israel would have learned their lesson—but no! They reach the other side of the sea and moan and groan that things were better in Egypt. At least they had enough to eat there. Why did Moses drag them out to this forsaken wilderness in the first place? This is supposed to be better?

Let's face it. With their attitude, they're asking for a major time out. So they get one. God gives them some time to think—40 years, to be precise. During that time they wander in a nomadic life around a wilderness. How do they know where to go? A pillar of cloud leads them by day and a pillar of fire guides them by night. The Israelites spend 40 years learning that life means moving in response to a stimulus. Over and over, they pick it up, pack it up and move on out.

In the New Testament, the disciples listen to the instructions of Jesus as he ascends to his place with the Father.

Do not leave Jerusalem, but wait for the gift my Father promised, which you have heard me speak about. . .But you will receive power when the Holy Spirit comes on you; and you will be my witnesses in Jerusalem, and in all Judea and Samaria, and to the ends of the earth.

—Acts 1:4, 8

So the disciples gather and experience the wonderful in-filling of the Spirit, go out proclaiming the Good News in various languages, and see 3,000 people come into the kingdom. Everything is so wonderful they want to camp right where they are. Why mess with a good thing? But Jesus had told them they were to spread this message throughout the world, not just in Jerusalem. They need to be on the move. When persecution arises, that is the stimulus necessary to get them going. Acts 8 tells us the disciples were scattered throughout Judea and Samaria. Before long, we read of their adventures in lands even further away: Antioch, Ephesus, Philippi. This movement was one sign that the early church was alive.

RESPIRATION

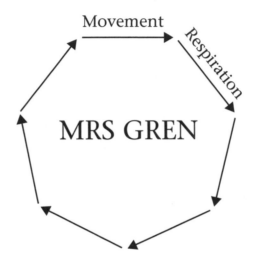

Respiration is not synonymous with breathing. Every cell in your body has built-in "powerhouses" called mitochondria that release energy. These powerhouses depend on oxygen brought into the body through breathing. So breathing is absolutely necessary for respiration to take place, and the respiration process is essential for energy to be released so the body can function and take another breath.

From time to time God visits his people and pours out his Spirit. In the Old and New Testaments, the same word is used to describe God's visitation. The Hebrew *ruach* and Greek *pneuma* both mean "breathe." God breathes on his people. God's Spirit is the same as his breath. In the same way that our breathing oxygen releases energy in our bodies, God's breathing into us releases the energy of his Spirit in our lives. God breathed into a lump of clay on the sixth day of creation and Adam came to life. We need God to breathe into us and bring us to life.

Have you ever seen a petulant child decide to hold his breath until his parents gave in and let him have his way? The child doesn't know he will pass out if he doesn't breathe (so his threat isn't all that threatening), and that his body's reflexes will push him to breathe even if he thinks he doesn't want to.

> God wants the very power of heaven to be loosed in our lives, and it comes by spiritual respiration.

Why do we sometimes resist spiritual breath? It takes more effort to resist breathing than to just do it! God is ready to breathe into us, yet we lock our lips shut. When we do that, God has to take drastic action to get us breathing again. God wants the very power of heaven to be loosed in our lives, and it comes by spiritual respiration.

Prayer is the breath of God filling us up again. We need to breathe deeply of the breath of God. In doing so, we will discover that the energy of God to complete the task at hand is released within us. But that is not in our nature, is it? When we are overwhelmed and don't seem to have the time to do all that is on our plate for the day, what is the first thing we forsake? A time of prayer, right? John Wesley, the great English reformer, knew that if he was to possibly tackle what the day held, he had to begin with prayer. If the agenda that day was especially full, he scheduled even more time for prayer. In Germany, Martin Luther did the same. In fact, Luther described his basic relationship with God as breathing.

I was a pastor planting a new church in Arizona when I first went through the LifeShapes course. As I sat and listened to Mike's incredible teaching, the series on MRS GREN really caught my attention, especially in regards to respiration. My new congregation and church staff had spent months getting all revved up to make something amazing happen. We spent so much time gearing up for the future and envisioning the amazing blessings that God was sure to pass along to us that we forgot to take the time to catch our breath. We were so worked up that we were hyperventilating. What happens when you hyperventilate? You pass out. Our brand new church was about to pass out from thinking too much about our breathing.

—*PASTOR KURT*

We are talking about normal healthy breathing, not hyperventilating. Today's Christian community has a strange continuum when it comes to spiritual breathing. On one end, you have someone taking a gulp of air every two minutes or so, just enough to stay alive but not really do anything else. Then there are those who suck in air as if it were going to cease to exist any minute now. These people soon get air-sick and need to lie down.

A third kind of breather gets it right: the runner. Someone who is in shape and can run great distances has developed a discipline in breathing. A natural, deep breath refreshes the runner's entire body with every inhalation, and clears the lungs with every exhalation.

We need to respire. We need to breathe in God. You're not thinking about breathing right now, are you? If you are, something is not right! Walking with God should be as automatic as the respiratory process. We need to learn what it means to walk in the Spirit, as Paul puts it. Walk and breathe at the same time. Can you do it?

Do you long to be spiritually fit? You must run after God. If you want to run after God you will have to learn to breathe deeply of his breath.

SENSITIVITY

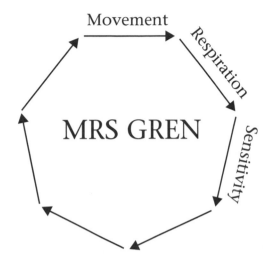

Movement

Respiration

MRS GREN

Sensitivity

Your body is not a bunch of independent parts randomly stuck together. It all works as one unit. That's the way God made you. Living organisms move according to stimuli. Our sensory organs, which have zillions of receptor cells, detect the stimulation and tell the brain there's something out there, and the brain tells the muscles to get moving or else!

In Egypt, Pharaoh hardened his heart to the Lord. After a while God said, "Okay, you want a hard heart? I'll give you one." Centuries later, Paul wrote to Timothy about people whose consciences had been "seared" (1 Tim. 4:2). They had said "No" to their consciences so many times that they lost all sensitivity to what was right.

Paul uses amazing language sometimes. He says, "I long after you all in the bowels of Jesus Christ" (Philippians 1:8, KJV). What is that about? Paul uses a word that literally refers to the intestines. In his time, it was also the word that meant the seat of emotions, what we might call the "heart." It's contemporary language for "I'm speaking to you with all of the passion that

I feel. I feel what you're feeling." When Paul writes to Philemon, he uses the same word, essentially saying, "refresh my guts" (Philemon 20). Because of the way the body works, we often feel a little tension in the stomach. Paul is saying, "I'm tense, and you make me relax."

> The human body has multiple senses, and so does the body of Christ.

Sensitivity is important in the kingdom. The human body has multiple senses, and so does the body of Christ. The more senses that are active, the more we will see the needs around us and be moved to respond. The pastoral, sensitive, caring side of what God wants to do in and through us is expressed through our spiritual receptor cells. Watch that your senses are not so dulled that you don't feel the pain and joy of people around you.

GROWTH

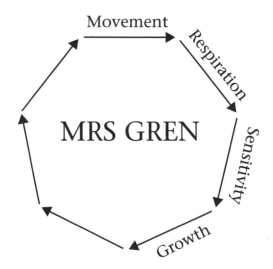

Movement
Respiration
MRS GREN
Sensitivity
Growth

Kids hate it when adults say, "Wow, you've really grown!" As if that were a surprise. Can't you just see the eyeballs rolling now? Kids grow; it's normal, it's what we expect. When they don't grow, we panic. Growth is a natural process to living things. Yet we marvel over it.

Growth doesn't happen at a steady upward pace. We don't see growth every day. Growth comes through the natural rhythms of life. Kids hit plateaus, then they shoot up and it seems like they've grown three inches overnight.

> Growth comes through the natural rhythms of life.

Are you growing? Sometimes it's hard to tell. But growth must be happening in a living being. When you stop growing, you die. It's that simple.

We are not told to work for our growth. God is the one who causes us to grow. (Look at 1 Corinthians 3:6-9 and Colossians 2:19—God makes us to grow.) But there are things we need to do to create a growing environment, both individually and corporately. If the other six aspects of MRS GREN are operating properly, growth will occur. So let's move on to the last three principles of MRS GREN.

CHAPTER 21

WE'RE ALIVE!

MRS GREN is about life and Jesus talks about life constantly. We are biological creatures and Jesus does not ignore this. As a matter of fact, many—if not most—of his stories and teachings deal with our bodies and their needs—food, clothing, shelter. As his followers today, we are still constrained in these bodies and have the same needs as the disciples two thousand years ago. Jesus has not forgotten how challenging daily life can be for us humans.

At the same time we must realize that our bodies and our spirits are intricately intertwined. This was a lesson Jesus tried to teach the Pharisees when he healed the paralytic (Luke 5:17-26) and obviously, as you read the numerous current articles about the connection between faith, prayer, and health, it a concept that modern man is reinvestigating. Jesus spent much of his ministry time on earth healing hurting and misshapen bodies, knowing that as he was doing this, he was touching their spirits as well.

We are living in times of critical change. The landscape is changing all around us: culturally, spiritually, corporately and individually. During these times

> Our bodies and our spirits are intricately intertwined.

of change, many will resist—we should know by now that resistance is futile. A synonym for futile is fruitless; producing no result and serving no useful purpose—that is *not* the mark of a passionate life! The seven signs of life represented by MRS GREN can help you understand how to remain healthy and fruitful even as the world changes around you. Let's continue to look at how the principles of MRS GREN can be applied to spiritual life.

REPRODUCTION

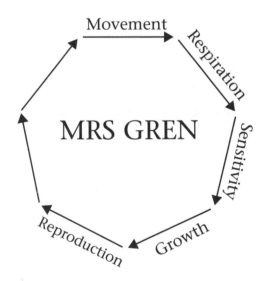

Reproduction is different from growth in that it is a multiplication of the whole organism, not simply growing new cells. All living things reproduce by bringing together two disparate elements and then fusing them together into a new element. A sperm and an egg, living cells unto themselves, come together to form a new organism. The new organism has similar traits and appearance as their "donors," the sperm and egg. Reproduction has taken place.

Created order seems to have a mechanism that prevents unhealthy specimens from being multiplied. The unhealthy ones generally don't reproduce; the healthy ones carry on the species. It is the goal of a species to create a healthy next generation, the most important target of their lives. Notice the language that Jesus uses in John 21 when he re-commissions Peter. He doesn't tell Peter to take care of the ones who have the most money or to look after the adults. He says, "Feed my lambs." The lambs are the little ones, the next generation.

For kingdom work, creating a healthy next generation of believers is the most important target we have. We are not just concerned with our own growth, but in obeying Jesus' command to go and make disciples throughout the world.

EXCRETION

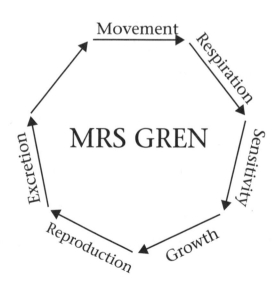

"Okay," you say. "I can see how the other six biological processes can be applied to the my life in God. But not excretion. That's just gross!" Wrong.

Our bodies are not the only things that build up a collection of junk throughout the day. Our hearts do too. We build up a sediment of sin and we need to get rid of it. We empty our hearts of this unhealthy stuff through the process of repentance. If we do not get rid of these sins, they will act just like toxins do in the human body, causing illness and eventually, death.

> We build up a sediment of sin and we need to get rid of it.

Jesus made it clear: Forgive others so God can forgive you. Grudge-bearing can be dangerous to your physical health as well—increased blood pressure, hormonal changes, cardiovascular disease and impaired brain functions, including memory loss. Not excreting what others have done to us is just as unhealthy as not getting rid of our own sins.

In John 13 Jesus washes the feet of his disciples. He says, "A person who has had a bath needs only to wash his feet; his whole body is clean." In other words, "You've been made clean already by the word I've spoken to you, but you need to let me wash your feet. They're dirty." We have to get rid of the stuff that would become toxic to our bodies if we don't eliminate it.

This is one of the reasons Jesus is so clear about ways to deal with relationships. In Matthew 18, he doesn't tell us to go tell the pastor or a best friend if we have something against another person. He sends us straight to that person. If the person won't listen, take a couple of witnesses. Take it to the whole church if you have to. That's how important it is to get relational toxins cleaned up.

If you don't excrete in your natural life, aside from looking really nasty and feeling very uncomfortable, you will die. That's a medical fact. Toxins build up within you and cause vital organs to stop working. Eventually your

Just like all moms, I'm concerned about my kids' health. Not too much candy when they were children; regular check-ups and immunizations through their school years; and now that they are teenagers, a healthy diet and exercise. After all, isn't that what a good mother does? The principles of MRS GREN made me realize that I should be giving as much attention to their spiritual health as I do their physical and emotional health. Have I taught them to pray? Do they know how to study the Bible? Can they make their own choices as a follower of Jesus? I should be discipling my own kids!

—A MOTHER OF TWO

entire body shuts down—permanently. The writer of Hebrews calls these toxins building up within us "the root of bitterness" (Heb. 12:15). We are told to remove it—rip it out.

NUTRITION

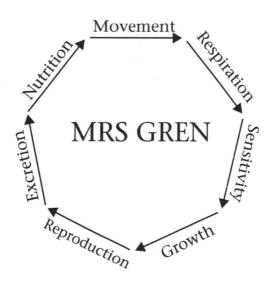

Finally we have nutrition. All living things must take in nutrients or they will die. In this era of carb-free this and fat-free that, we have an even greater awareness of proper nutrition. For the spiritual diet, there is but one main course. "I am the bread of life," declares Jesus (John 6:48). To live, we must dine on his words, his actions, his commands. We can break this down even further.

When Jesus met with the woman at the well (John 4), he led her to discover that he himself was living water. If she drank from the water that he offered, she would never be thirsty again. As she marveled at what he was saying, the disciples showed up. They had gone off to a nearby village to buy food. When they came back, they offered some to Jesus.

"I have food to eat that you know nothing about," he said (John 4:32). The disciples wondered just where he got this food and what it was. Someone must have offered Jesus food while they were gone. Perhaps they were jealous, thinking it was probably better than what they had to eat. Then Jesus spelled it out clearly for them.

"My food is to do the will of him who sent me," he told them.

Obeying God is our nutrition. When we obey the commands of Jesus, our souls are fed. We feel full and fulfilled.

Without nutrition, you will die. There is no way around that. In the same way, believers will die if there is not a regular feeding on Jesus, the very Word of God. We must clearly and consistently proclaim his teachings. But we can't stop there. We must obey his commands to get our fill of nutrition vital for our growth.

There she is—MRS GREN.

CHAPTER 22

A PERSONAL CHECK-UP

Have you ever had an ingrown toenail? It can be amazingly painful! Our nails are supposed to grow out naturally and when they do, we don't give them a second thought. But when the natural growth of a nail is inhibited, it can become inflamed and infected and annoyingly irritating. Most ingrown nails are found on the feet of Westerners who insist on cramming their toes into ill-fitting shoes. How does a nail become ingrown? It improperly responds to outward pressure, inhibiting its natural growth.

As a Christian, have you become spiritually ingrown? Are there areas of your life where you have misdirected attention and energy or responded inappropriately to outside pressures? This is an unhealthy state of affairs. Left unattended, those areas of your life may fester, become diseased and cause you great pain. It's not enough to read Jesus' teachings—to know the kind of life he is offering us. We must make a conscious effort to compare our lives with the truths of Scripture. We need regular check-ups and MRS GREN can help.

SELF-CHECK

Doctors say that most cancers can be completely cured if they are found in time. Thus, we are taught how to check our bodies for potential signs of cancer or other disease so we can catch it, cure it and live. Just as you conduct self-examinations on your physical body, you can perform spiritual self-exams. Becoming aware of the seven processes of MRS GREN teaches us how to make a thorough exam.

Susan squirms when her cardiologist asks the inevitable question: "What's the most vigorous activity you've done in the last six months?" Images flash through Susan's mind. That seven-mile hike she thought about last summer. No, that didn't happen. Swimming really just amounts to splashing around at the edge of the pool trying to stay out of the way of the kids' water basketball game. The treadmill gathers more dust than she wants to admit. "Walking vigorously" is all she can come up with. She hates that question. But it always makes her think about her activity choices. She may never run a marathon, but she can walk three miles every day. She can be active if she chooses to be.

Are you moving? Jesus says, "Come, follow me." Move. Grow. Don't become stagnant. We must be ready to do new things and to do the old things in new ways. This is **movement**, a vital sign that you are alive. God uses a variety of stimuli to prod us to move: Scriptures, sermons, prophecy, persecution. Our response should always be the same—move.

Second, what's your **respiration** rate? An asthma patient uses a "peak flow monitor" to see how much air the patient's lungs are moving. Air flow below a certain level requires immediate attention. In an asthmatic episode, breathing is painful or triggers a coughing fit, and the lungs never really feel full. Breathing is not automatic, it's labored. Physical energy is non-existent.

Are you letting God breathe into you? Are you breathing steadily, healthily, like the disciplined runner? Or are you hyperventilating and gasping for air? For spiritual energy we must be breathing in the breath of God through prayer. Think of

> Take some deep breaths of God's Spirit and see what a powerhouse he becomes in your life.

prayer as a peak flow monitor for your spiritual respiration. Are you spending regular time in prayer? Are you getting enough of the breath of God? If not, don't be surprised when you lack spiritual energy. Take some deep breaths of God's Spirit and see what a powerhouse he becomes in your life.

What about **sensitivity**? In Ephesians 4 Paul explains the fivefold gifts that serve as the foundation of ministry—to each other, as well as to the world. God's kingdom needs people who will be sensitive to hearing others, listening actively, and then instructing them on how to proceed. These are our teachers. Those sensitive in speech, being gifted to share the good news on any occasion, are the evangelists. And the ones who can sniff out staleness and knows it is time to move forward are the apostles, sensitive to the move of God to explore new territory for the kingdom.

God wants us all to be sensitive to his stimuli so that we will move and act as he directs. We need those who touch the needs and pains of others, the pastors who can laugh with those who laugh and cry with those cry. We need those who are sensitive to sight, in this case foresight given by God. These are the prophets.

Are your receptors cells working? Or have they become dull and

---

FOR MORE ON MINISTRY ROLES, SEE THE PENTAGON, CHAPTER 16

indistinct? Do you see and feel and hear the pain of people around you? Do you see and hear and feel the joy of people around you? Do you sense God's nudging when he wants you to do something, or is your conscience seared and your heart hardened?

Are you **growing**? Look back at where you were a month ago, six months ago, a year ago. How far have you come? Maybe you'll even surprise yourself with how much you've grown. You may also reflect on a plateau of spiritual growth. At the time you may have thought things were pretty flat spiritually. In retrospect, you may be able to see how God was preparing you for a growth spurt that would take you into a new stage of your spiritual life.

Are you **reproducing** and helping others to grow? The need is great.

Look at Europe. Children, teenagers and young adults don't attend church any longer. Why is that? Christians in Europe have forsaken the re-production of themselves into a new generation. There really isn't a "next generation" of Christians in Europe. Perhaps the older generations of Christians were not healthy, so they have not procreated. God will do a new thing—spark new growth—in Europe, but it is not going to come in the natural order of things. Our primary cry must be for the children to come. We must say with the psalmist:

> *Even when I am old and gray,*
> > *do not forsake me, O God,*
> *till I declare your power to the next*
> > *generation,*
> *your might to all who are to come.*

—Psalm 71:18

In our spiritual life, God takes our words (sharing the Good News of God's forgiveness in the person of Jesus) and fuses them with the heart of someone open to the Good News to make a new spirit—one that is alive, born from above. This is reproduction on the spiritual level. One Christian has become two. From these two will come four. A small group will form, and soon it will be multiplied into more small groups, forming a church.

How are you doing in bringing forth children for the kingdom? Is reproduction important to you? It should be—it's a signal that you are alive.

Excretion is a sensitive subject. We don't like to admit we have all that crud piling up inside us. In our self-righteousness, we're quick to see the offenses of others toward us rather than our own sin. The guy who cuts us off in traffic is an idiot. The umpire who called that third strike is blind and incompetent. How could so-and-so fall for that stupid sales pitch? We compare our best moments to the worst habits of other people, and we come out looking pretty good. Like the Pharisee, we thank God that we are not like the tax collector. But sin is sin, and it's all toxic. It's got to go.

Jesus wants us get rid of the bitter toxins, especially unforgiveness. This is such an important part of having a healthy spirit that Jesus includes this in his model prayer. "Forgive us as we forgive" is something we need to pray daily.

Finally, what are you eating? Are you feeding on Jesus? Are you eating regular, healthy meals for proper spiritual **nutrition**, or just trying to grab something on the run and not being all that careful about your spiritual diet? A church service a couple of times a month. Maybe a little devotional booklet when you think of it—which is not all that often if you're honest. A quick prayer over your lunch if other Christians are watching, but not if unbelievers are watching.

FOR MORE ON PRAYER, SEE THE HEXAGON, CHAPTERS 18 AND 19

> We can't live on spiritual junk food.

Changing your diet is not an easy thing. Ask anyone who has tried to lose 20 pounds, eliminate salt to lower blood pressure, or go low-fat to bring down cholesterol. The healthy stuff takes more time to prepare, more time to shop for, maybe even more money to buy. It takes effort and constant awareness. But the long-term benefits are enormous.

Jesus is the bread that fills us up. We can't live on spiritual junk food. We must come to the table he lays before us and eat heartily of the meal he offers.

GROWING STRONGER

Do you see where we are going with this? LifeShapes is not a course that you do once, get a certificate to hang on your wall, and forget it. It really is all about life. Examining yourself using MRS GREN, you will see where potential life-threatening problems are.

Each of the LifeShapes calls for movement.

When a *kairos* moment prompts you to enter the Circle, you move through repentance to faith.

The Semi-Circle calls for us to move back and forth from abiding to fruitfulness and back to abiding.

Your Up relationship with God (seen in the Triangle) moves you to have In and Out relationships as well.

In the Square, leaders help learners move through each side in sequence, or the whole process will fail.

If your base ministry in the Pentagon is pastor, you will constantly move through the other four roles as phase ministries.

The Lord's Prayer, LifeShape Six, is a model prayer where each of the six parts moves through all of the others.

And in the Octagon still to come, we will find the Person of Peace and invite him or her to walk (move) with us.

Go through each of the seven processes of life in this way, checking your own pulse. When you find an area you have been neglecting, give it more attention. Don't wait until disease sets in and you need emergency room care. Exercise preventive self-care so that your spiritual remains vibrant and Spirit-filled.

CHAPTER 23

A LIFESTYLE OF OUTREACH

O h, no. Eight sides. These shapes are getting complicated."

Don't let the fact that the Octagon has eight sides put you off. We're not going to load you down with eight major theological lessons or eight principles with eight sub-points you need to memorize, it's going to be much simpler than that. We want the Octagon to remind you of sharing the Good News, the only task Jesus left us with. And there is one main message of the Octagon: Find the Person of Peace.

Our outward relationships are not just to be occasional outreach projects or evangelism programs. We are to live a lifestyle of mission, evangelism, and service. Jesus explained his mission to his disciples as "the reason I have come" (Mark 1:38). He spoke of sending his followers as the Father had sent him (John 20:21). He commissioned them as disciple-makers (Matt. 28:19). He described them as his witnesses in continually expanding spheres until their message reached the ends of the earth (Acts 1:8).

This biblical strategy for evangelism is the focus of the Octagon.

THE PERSON OF PEACE

So often we feel beaten up by the strategy of evangelism we take on. Sometimes we try too hard to drag in rather than reach out. Jesus taught his disciples a strategy of evangelism that didn't depend on programs or budgets or buildings or drawing a crowd. As Jesus commissioned the 72 disciples to go ahead of him, proclaiming the coming of kingdom of God, he gave them directions for how to proceed:

When you enter a house, first say, "Peace to this house." If a man of peace is there, your peace will rest on him; if not, it will return to you.

—Luke 10:5–6

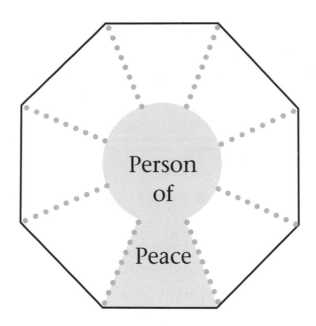

Jesus tells his disciples—and, thus, is telling us today—that as we walk through life in this world, we should be on the look-out for a Person of Peace. Who is this Person of Peace, and how will we recognize the Person of Peace?

Very simply, a Person of Peace is one who is prepared to hear the message of the kingdom and the King. The Person of Peace is ready to receive what God will give you to say at that moment. This should be our prayer as we venture forth each day. "Lord, bring into my path today a Person of Peace, and give me the grace and courage to speak your words to this person." Someone who is not a Person of Peace will not receive what you have to say. Don't feel obliged to belabor the issue. Jesus says to shake the dust off your feet and move on. You can study up on all the objections people have to Christianity and how to answer them. You can be ready with points one, two and three. You can be persistent because you really believe this person needs to know Jesus. But in the end, no amount of coercion on your part can make someone become a Person of Peace. That's the job of the Holy Spirit; he alone can prepare a heart to hear the Gospel. Our job is to have our spiritual eyes open, looking for a Person of Peace to cross our paths. We must keep in mind five things as we look for the person of peace in our lives.

> "Lord, bring into my path today a Person of Peace, and give me the grace and courage to speak your words to this person."

Time

Jesus precedes sending out the disciples with an exhortation that there are specific times and places when the harvest is ripe. He links this discernment with an observation: Lift up your eyes. Not every section of society or subculture is equally ready and open to the Gospel. In some contexts we need to sow, while in others we should be prepared to reap. Part of our mission is to have God's perspective showing us where there is a spiritual openness (John 4:34-38).

Harvest is just one season of several that rotate through the years. You can't harvest at planting time or during the main growing season. You have to wait for the right time to bring the crop in. Checking the corn every day to see if it's gotten any taller doesn't bring the harvest time any sooner.

Jesus says the harvest is plentiful. There is always an opportunity to see people come to Christ when it is the right time for those people. For instance, you may have a better harvest with your neighborhood than among your coworkers. So concentrate on bringing in the harvest in your neighborhood while you wait out the growing season at work.

Disciples through the ages have made the mistake of thinking that if they just work harder the harvest will come sooner. Jesus doesn't say that. In John 4, he says, "Open your eyes and look; the harvest is there." In other words, go back to the learning Circle and go through the steps of Observe, Reflect and Discuss to find out where the harvest is. Where is the greatest level of receptivity at this stage of your life and in the places where you spend your time?

> Disciples through the ages have made the mistake of thinking that if they just work harder the harvest will come sooner.

When I (Mike) was a pastor in Brixton, what we did working in the deepest inner city of London was to go around and ask people what they thought we should do. We knocked on doors and surveyed them. We wanted to find out what was going on. So we asked questions about what the church should be doing in the community and what were the big issues that the church could get involved with. We had no hidden agenda. It wasn't a trick to try to sneak in the four spiritual laws. It was a simple questionnaire that helped us observe the receptivity of people in the neighborhood. We found people who said, "It's the children and young people." Others said, "The big problem is the trash on the streets."

So we went back and prayed. This was in the 80s, and around that time, Graham Kendrick was beginning the March for Jesus movement. So we started a praise and litter march through our community once a month. A lot of people came to Christ because they saw a metaphor of the kingdom right there in front of them. They saw the church at work.

Team

Jesus always sent his disciples on mission ahead of him in pairs. A team always had a minimum of two. We also see this principle in the ministry of Paul. He constantly refers to his teammates—Barnabas, Silas, Timothy, Titus, Luke. Our inward relationships lead to our outward ministry. We are not called to go alone.

Why teams? It's simple, really. Ecclesiastes 4:9 says, "Two are better than one, because they have a good return for their work." So if you sense the Spirit's push to witness to your friends, look around. Who is on your team? Who can be with you in a social setting where it would be appropriate to share? Who can promise to pray for you consistently as you answer this call? Who can help you discern when the time is right to speak?

Target

Jesus is strategic in his outreach. He knows he could not be everywhere at once, and neither could his disciples. He focused their outreach on the lost sheep of the house of Israel (Matt. 10:6) and warned them against being distracted by those not ready to receive their message (Luke 9:5 and 10:4).

Jesus doesn't tell his disciples to stand on a soap box on the street corner and start preaching. Rather, he says to look for the Person of Peace. Look for the person who is receptive to you personally, the person for whom it is harvest time right now.

FOR MORE ON IN, SEE THE TRIANGLE, CHAPTER 10

> Look for the person for whom it is harvest time right now.

As you look for opportunities to share the good news of the kingdom of heaven, look for people who are open to you and your message. Concentrate on these receptive people of peace, and don't force dialogue or relationship where it does not flow naturally. This is a liberating principle, because it means that we're looking for people who like us! How hard is that? You know people who like you and people who don't. Don't spend your time trying to get people to like you. They'll just think you're even more strange. Instead, find someone who likes you and start there.

When people finally understand this principle, the lights go on. They start to say, "I've got a Person of Peace at work" or "My neighbor is a Person of Peace." Evangelism isn't about how many notches you can get on your Bible—you don't have to reach hundreds or thousands or hundreds of thousands to be successful. Jesus wants you to reach the one he has put in your path today and it just may be that little kid who smiles at you from the sidewalk and wants to know your name. Start there!

Task

The disciple's assignment is to share the Good News of the kingdom with the Person of Peace, whenever and wherever that person is found. How do we recognize the Person of Peace? According to the instructions Jesus gave his disciples in Matthew 10 and Luke 10, the Person of Peace will:

- Welcome you. If he does not, you are to "shake the dust off your feet" as you leave his home (Matt. 10:14).
- Listen to you. Those who listen to you are listening to Jesus (Luke 10:16).

- Serve or support you. We must allow a Person of Peace to serve us (Matt. 10:10).

Trouble

If the teacher is not received, Jesus said, the students should not expect a warm welcome either. As you go out into the world looking for the Person of Peace and sharing the Good News of kingdom of God, expect trouble. Many are not yet ready to hear the message, and they will react strongly against what they perceive as intolerance or insensitivity on your part. As for this happening, know that it is not a question of "if" but "when." What can we do with people at the height of spiritual resistance? It is often in our nature to try and find the most difficult person in a group to try and bring to Christ, especially if we are in a close relationship with them. But unless Christ has prepared them to receive his love, our aggression will be unfruitful, perhaps even damaging. Use this time as an opportunity to back away from the trouble. Commit yourselves to prayer over this person and set an example of love toward them. In the words of St. Francis, "Preach the Gospel, and use words if you have to." By living in love and prayer, God will take our actions and prepare the ground for the seeds to be planted when the time is right.

RICH—A PERSON OF PEACE

I was a soccer player on a university team. During practice sessions, I often played up against a guy named Dave. We got to know each other, and I enjoyed playing against him because he was always encouraging. He never swore and was always really friendly. Most of my experience with soccer players at school convinced me that these guys were foul-mouthed and bad-tempered, so Dave was definitely different.

We became friends, talked about stuff, met for coffee and things like that. He seemed genuinely interested in me. Around Christmas time, tickets went on sale for the Christians in Sports dinner. I bought one from Dave because it looked like a great meal for a cheap price, and also because I liked the guys who were going. I found out later that the three guys who were going were all Christians. I'd never really had any deep spiritual questions before, but I went along and enjoyed it.

An athlete got up and gave his testimony to about 200 people who were there, telling how he'd come to know the Lord in the last year. That really struck me. I knew this guy and liked him. He was amazingly honest and brave to share this stuff. The way he talked and the way he led his life just all made sense. He seemed to have a peace and a joy that I wanted. I thought, "This is right. I should live like this."

When everything was over, I found Dave and told him I wanted to know more. He suggested that I come to his house to talk. For the next six weeks or so, another guy and I went to Dave's house and ate with him and Jim (his housemate). We watched the Alpha video and talked about the questions we had.

It was very relaxed. Dave and Jim let us ask everything from basic to deep questions. Dave gave me a Bible, and I started to read it a little. These two months built up my knowledge of God, and by the end I believed in my head about Jesus and God. Dave invited me to go to church, so I went. I was blown away, but also strangely drawn and kept going with Dave.

After I'd been going about three months, I was in my car one Sunday morning and started humming "Amazing Grace" quite randomly. The moment passed as quickly as it had come. That evening I went to a service. At the end, a saxophone player came to center stage and started to play "Amazing Grace." I knew he was playing it for me. That was the moment that God captured my heart. This Jesus I had learned about in my head and believed in was real and he knew me. He was there in the morning when I hummed, and he was there in the evening when the sax played. He wanted my heart as well as my head. It just blew me away. I made my way to the front of the church and gave my life to the Lord.

The next week I heard a presentation about a kids' club. I went down and signed up to help. The newfound love I had for God compelled me to action. I wanted to say "thank you" in the way I lived. Now I've been involved in ministry with kids for six years. I'm going to keep doing it until God tells me something different.

Dave was an usher at my wedding, and my wife and I led the prayers at his wedding. He is a constant source of love and encouragement to me. I model how I am with my non-Christian friends based on the way Dave was with me.

The Spirit of God will put people in your path who need to hear the Good News. You won't have to look very far. But you do have to have your eyes open and be willing to turn your head from side to side. You do have to be open to your day taking a detour if an opportunity arises to share the kingdom news.

CHAPTER 24

WHERE IS THE PERSON OF PEACE?

*J*ust in case an eight-sided shape still feels a bit intimidating, we've made all the sides start with the same letter: P. All these "P" words will help you understand the principles at work as you have your eyes open for opportunities to share kingdom news with your Person of Peace. These principles are not in a sequential order. Any of these opportunities can happen at any time—if you are looking for and recognizing them.

FINDING YOUR PERSON OF PEACE

Presence Evangelism

Presence Evangelism happens when you are simply present in a situation with an individual or group. Pretty obvious, really. Where you are right now is always an opportunity to model Jesus, acting as he would act, speaking as he would speak. As you show kindness and speak encouragement, your eyes may be opened to a Person of Peace who is right there with you. Perhaps you are in a committee meeting and you speak in a positive way when others are complaining. After the meeting another committee member comes up to you and thanks you for remaining positive. This could be a Person of Peace making himself known. You have an opportunity to share

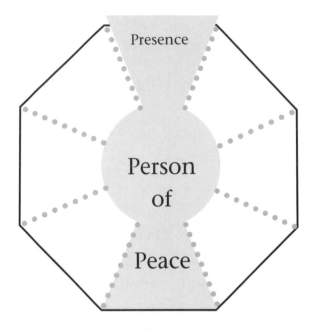

why you are upbeat just because you are present in that situation. As the wise man said, "Wherever you go, there you are." And wherever you are may be an opportunity to meet with a Person of Peace.

Years ago my wife, Sally, and I (Mike) were driving in our old car in Cambridge when she saw someone on the sidewalk. She was pretty sure it was someone she knew, so we looked a little closer. Sure enough, it was Helen, someone she had known years ago. I urged Sally to get out and talk to Helen. At first she was hesitant. It had been a long time since they'd seen each other, perhaps it would be too awkward. "You never, know, it might be the Lord," I told Sally as I pulled the car over to the curb. I really didn't give her much of a choice.

Sally got out and said "hello" to Helen—who greeted her like a long lost hero, with far more enthusiasm and receptivity than Sally expected. Helen had just arrived in Cambridge to start a nursing job. She was very glad to see

When our neighbor's husband died, I wanted to reached out to her in love and support. I made myself available to her and soon found I had a new friend. As a result of being present in this woman's life, she became more receptive to the message of Jesus Christ. I started to disciple my new friend and she began to attend church. Recently she sent me a note thanking me and my husband for helping her grow in her faith. If I had stuck to my own little group of friends, I would have missed out on making a cherished new friend and helping to welcome a new sister in Christ into the family of God.

—*MARY*

a familiar face, even from long ago. Sally explained that we were in Cambridge because of my work as a pastor.

Helen didn't know anyone in town. She came to church the next week. Soon after that, Billy Graham came to town with an evangelistic crusade. Helen came with us to the crusade meeting and became a Christian as a result.

Sally was very glad she had gotten out of the car that day.

Passing Relationships

We have passing relationships with people we meet only once or twice. The clerk at the gas station. A stranger standing in line at the bank. The person you happen to sit next to on a plane. The postman dropping off your mail. Most likely, even if it's clear this is a Person of Peace at that moment, you are probably not going to lead this person into a personal relationship with Christ in that brief encounter. But God may use

You may be called on to plant a seed or to water what has already been planted.

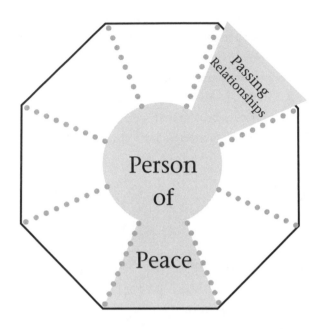

you to take the person closer to that point. Paul said that some people plant, some people water, and God gives the harvest (1 Cor. 3:6). In a passing relationship, you may be called on to plant a seed or to water what has already been planted. Just because you do not see the end result does not mean you are not a vital part of the process.

Permanent Relationships

You have permanent relationships with your family and with close friends. If a passing relationship is like a sprint, a permanent relationship is a marathon. You are with these people often, and for extended periods of time. It is important that you do not force the Gospel message on these people when they are not ready. You may have to wait for a long time before he or she is

> God is never in a hurry, and he is never late.

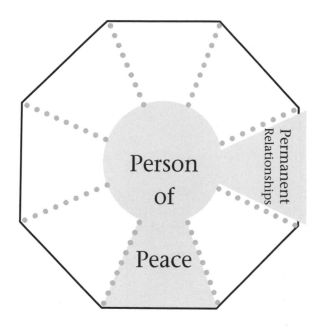

a Person of Peace for you. Until that time comes, the person's heart may not be ready to hear you.

We often have the hardest time sharing our faith with those closest to us. Perhaps this is due in part to our impatience. We want so much for them to live the incredible kingdom life that we are experiencing that we rush them toward salvation before God has prepared them to hear us. Pray, wait and watch. God is never in a hurry, and he is never late.

Proclamation

You don't have to be a great orator—proclamation is not just for preachers. You don't have to be a prolific writer—proclamation is not just for authors. Your audience doesn't have to be large and no one is asking you to stand on a street corner with a placard. To proclaim means to give outward indication of something—to show others openly and publicly the kingdom life.

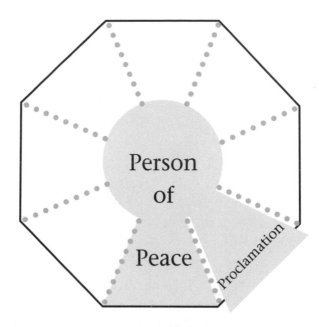

We should all look for opportunities to proclaim the Gospel to those who are not believers. It's simply declaring the message that Jesus shared: Repent and believe. This could even be with one person you are talking with. By speaking a gentle word testifying to Christ's work in your life, you can use proclamation to identify a Person of Peace. Does the person seem to respond to what you say? Enter into a relationship with this person, or connect the person with others who can walk with the Person of Peace in the initial stages of discipleship. This is what evangelism really is: inviting a person to walk the walk of faith, not just pray a prayer.

Preparation

Preparation is similar to cultivating soil and planting seed in advance of the harvest. Your words will be one turn of a person's soil. Someone else comes along and, sensing an opportunity with a Person of Peace, turns the soil once again. The next week, the soil gets turned over one more time.

I met Kemi when we were both about 18. I was a Christian, but not very close to God at that stage in my life. When I became quite committed to my faith again, Kemi thought I had completely lost it. We were best friends; we talked about men, work, families, life in general but God was one area that we could not talk about. Still Kemi and I remained close friends over the next five years or so, even when we lived in different cities. Thank goodness for phone calls and emails!

As the years passed, I just kept on being myself with Kemi, loving her and enjoying our friendship. One day Kemi called me and said, "Tell me everything. I need to know it all right now." Kemi had met some other Christians whose lives had been radically changed by their faith, and she was blown away. She said, "It's like I'm walking down the street and I hear someone calling my name. I'm not where I need to be, but I don't want to be where I've been." I was overjoyed. After all this time, the seed had grown and Kemi was ready.

—*KATIE*

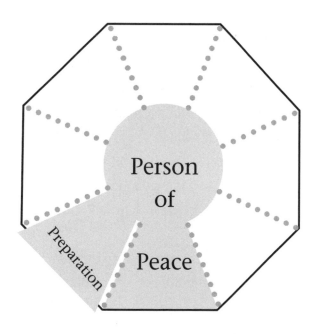

Then yet another believer comes and plants seed. A few more come and water the seed. None of these individual workers sees what the others have done, and perhaps none of them will be there for the harvest. But all have had a hand in making a disciple.

Chris was involved in a youth ministry team and was looking for ways to empower the Christian youth he worked with to reach out to their non-Christian friends. They started up an informal soccer game. They just messed around after school, kicking the ball around and having fun together. The Christian kids began inviting their non-Christian friends, and soon about 30 boys were gathering every week after school to play soccer.

This was a comfortable way for the Christian boys to reach out. They weren't preaching; they were playing soccer. But they were also building friendships and creating a climate where it was safe for the non-Christian kids to ask questions. And they did ask questions. One boy got curious enough to go to church and soon became a Christian.

Chris and the other leaders decided to run a program that would let the kids explore questions about faith and learn who Jesus is. They invited all the boys who had been playing soccer, and they brought their friends as well. About 40 teenagers got involved in this program. Over the next few weeks, 12 of them became Christians.

A few months later, Chris set up a formal soccer team made of Christians and non-Christian friends. They joined a local league. Now this team has set up a small group where other teenagers can talk about what it means to follow Christ.

Chris cultivated the soil until it was ready for planting, then watered patiently as the plant grew. Finally the harvest came!

Power

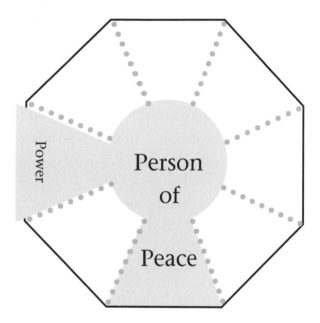

Jesus often used the power of God in miracles to reveal the Person of Peace. Praying for the sick and seeing a miraculous healing may reveal a Person of Peace. That person may be the one who was prayed for, or they could even be someone standing on the sidelines as an observer. Our God is an awesome God. He will do things to create awe in those who have yet to commit their hearts to him.

Marlene was helping at a Saturday night evangelistic service. This was the first time Marlene had done this and she was nervous. She had never led anyone to the Lord before. A woman came forward asking for prayer for healing from severe arthritic pain. As Marlene prayed with her for release from the pain, the woman looked up and said, "I have a confession." Marlene wasn't sure what to think, so she just let the woman continue. Clearly she had something on her mind that she wanted to say. Although her family thought she was a Christian, she considered herself an agnostic.

She really didn't know what she believed about God. Marlene spoke with her and the woman responded, praying for God's forgiveness. When they finished praying together, the woman's pain was gone—just gone! She had been powerfully healed at the moment of forgiveness. She walked into that service lost and hurting, she walked out found and healed.

We do not create these miracles, nor can we box God up and manipulate when and where miracles will occur. All we can do is be ready when they do happen. The Person of Peace may be revealed at any moment and we should be ready for that time.

Perception

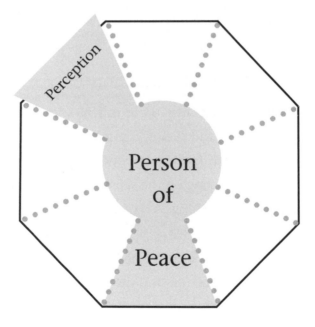

Suppose you are in a presence evangelism setting while golfing with three other people you just met on the first tee. As you complete your round and are shaking hands after the eighteenth hole, you ask yourself, "What is the temperature of the 'soil?' Is it hot, warm or cold?" If the temperature is cold—none of the people are showing any signs of being open to your sharing the Good News with them—move on. Shake the dust from your clear as it were, and wish them well. But if you sense any warmth in the soil, pursue a further relationship with that person. He or she may be a Person of Peace for you.

Perceptions can be false and misleading. That is why you need to be constantly in contact with the Holy Spirit as you try to discern a Person of Peace. The point of this principle is to open yourself up to observation, to become increasingly aware of when the Holy Spirit is leading you and to understand how to respond when you do become aware.

THE GREATEST EVANGELIST EVER

We've said more than once that Jesus was the wisest man who ever lived, as well as the best leader and teacher. It just makes sense that he would also be the best at evangelism. In his book *Permission Evangelism,* Michael Simpson looks at Jesus' interaction with the rich, young ruler (Mark 10) and sums it up this way:

> Christ was evangelizing, but it sure doesn't look like the way most people do it today. Even though it says Jesus loved him, he stood there and let the man walk away. Why did Christ not follow him when he walked away? Why didn't he try harder when this man seemed so eager? Why didn't Jesus 'get him saved' before addressing this difficult area of his life [his riches]?

Christ didn't run after the rich young ruler because he knew the young man's heart wasn't ready. Jesus knew and let him walk. Jesus never ran after anyone. Instead, he made himself available to those willing to wholeheartedly seek the Way to God, the Truth about God, and the Life found in God.*

LifeShapes is about learning what Jesus does, then doing the same in our lives. Jesus did not try to force open doors—he looked for the people who had their doors open, then he entered their world with his radical and life-changing call to follow him. If this is how Jesus shared the Gospel, why should we do it any differently?

The Person of Peace is someone God has prepared for the specific time and circumstances in which you meet the person. It is no good trying to force open doors that God has not opened, and we must not be distracted so that we miss the doors he has opened. This really is exciting news. Even in the one task we have been given—the assignment to go and make disciples—God does most of the work. Our main job is to walk through life with our eyes open and our ears listening to the Spirit as he reveals to us the Person of Peace.

MICHAEL SIMPSON, *PERMISSION EVANGELISM* (COLORADO SPRINGS: COOK COMMUNICATIONS MINISTRIES 2003), 51.

CHAPTER 25

So Now What?

A Circle of repentance and faith.

A Semi-circle of rest and work.

A Triangle of relationships.

A Square of priorities.

A Pentagon of ministry.

A Hexagon of prayer.

A Heptagon of life.

An Octagon of peace.

Eight shapes. We hope that you'll see these shapes all around you as you walk through your daily routine. And we hope that you'll never see any of these shapes again without thinking about their meaning in your life of discipleship.

Are we asking you to be running back and forth trying to keep all eight plates spinning fast enough that none of them will fall?

No.

People are drawn to particular shapes for various reasons—personal relationships, work circumstances, a season of life, personality or a dozen other things. You may decide the time is right for you to work out the Triangle in your life, focusing on Up, In and Out relationships. You may decide to take the familiar words of the Lord's Prayer, which perhaps you've been saying all your life, and find out what they really mean for your faith walk. You may find yourself in a situation where you are surrounded by People of Peace, and you know it's time to put those principles into action. Weeks or months or years from now you may feel God tugging at you to focus on another shape. Let the Spirit do his work in you and through you. Look to the Teacher. Follow.

"I DON'T KNOW WHAT'S OVER THERE."

CJ is a social teenage girl who is a marvel to watch when she's caring for young children. But she doesn't like new things. She has a tight circle of friends and is very content with that. When presented with the challenge to do something she hasn't tried before, even just going to a new restaurant, she'll come up with a handful of reasons why it's a bad idea. Her mother sometimes has to insist. She knows her daughter well enough to suggest activities she's fairly sure CJ would enjoy—if she would just tried them. Most of the time, CJ is glad she had the new experience. She's found something else she enjoys, but for CJ that first step is horrendously frightening.

> We can trust Jesus to take us to places he knows are right for us.

How many of us are like that in our faith walk? We want to follow Jesus—but in our own familiar ways, where we know what is supposed to happen next and how everything will feel. We're timid about new things, and Jesus definitely is leading us into new territory.

We can trust Jesus to take us to places he knows are right for us.

"Let me get ready first."

A woman said, "When I sit down at my desk, I'd almost rather spend the whole morning getting organized than actually getting down to work." She's not alone.

Let's not make discipleship more complicated than it is. In order to be a really good Christian, we act like we must maintain a minimum level of ministry activities, a certain number of hours of Bible study and prayer each day. A theological degree, of course, is important, maybe even more than one. To be a serious disciple, we tell ourselves, means setting goals and making plans for how we're going to get there, as if spiritual formation can be accomplished with a good management course.

In that context, eight shapes may not look so bad but it really all boils down to one point—learning from the Master. Look at what Jesus did. Look at what Jesus said. Then do that. The Spirit will help you know what each day's step is. Remember, a disciple is a *learner*, not a master, not an expert and not a pro. Be ready to keep on learning instead of focusing on the destination—because that day will never come. If you use up all your time and energy getting ready to be a serious disciple, you won't have any left for actually being a disciple.

"But I can't do that."

"Lord, I believe, but please don't send me to Africa." We laugh when we hear that, because the sentiment feels so familiar to all of us. We're afraid that being a disciple who is passionate about the kingdom of God means uprooting our whole lives to do something we're not very good at. After all, didn't the disciples leave their fishing nets to follow Jesus? Read that story again. "Follow me, and I will make you fishers of men." Jesus turned people who fished for fish into people who fished for other people. In other words, he accepted them as they were and used their abilities for the kingdom. He didn't say, "Put the nets away. Now you have to be a carpenter because that's the trade I learned." Jesus did not ask the disciples to be something they were not. But he did ask them to be everything God meant for them to be. He did ask them to step out of their comfort zones in faith. He did want them to catch the vision of the kingdom and be excited to do their part.

> Jesus did not ask the disciples to be something they were not.

Following Jesus does not mean a shy person suddenly has to become a public speaker at evangelistic gatherings. You don't automatically have to sign up to be a missionary on some forgotten island. It doesn't even mean you have to be in "full time Christian ministry." God created you, and God knows just how he wants to use you in spreading the Good News. Don't be so afraid that you'll have to go to Africa that you miss the calling God really does have for you today. Perhaps he just wants you to go over the back fence to find the Person of Peace he has prepared for you.

"I NEED TO CLEAR MY CALENDAR."

With a sigh, we look at our planners with stuff scribbled in every square and wonder when we'll have time to do this discipleship thing. Right?

Remember, we are human *beings*, not human *doings*. Following Jesus is about *being* like him. Discipleship is not one compartment of our lives—it is everything! We are whole beings. We don't separate out religious activities or times to practice being disciples. Jesus calls us to follow him with our whole lives. That means discipleship in the middle of sorting laundry, picking the kids up from school, during a business lunch, getting a haircut, putting dinner on the table, raking the leaves. Every-moment discipleship. Passionate discipleship.

"I don't know how to get started."

How do you get started taking a walk?

You decide you'd like to go for a walk. It begins with a decision. It may be motivated by an overly full holiday stomach, the guilt of a sedentary life, an impatient puppy, or the opportunity to be alone for a few minutes. Whatever the reason, you decide to take a walk. You may have to find your shoes and get a jacket out of the closet, but for the most part, you simply act on your decision and go out the front door. You might wave at the neighbors, or turn up a block you don't usually take. You look around at houses and notice the one with the new paint or the For Sale sign that wasn't there last week. You just keep taking the next step.

So how do you get started taking a faith walk?

You decide to go for a walk with Jesus. You find out where Jesus is going, and you want to go there with him. If you wander into an unfamiliar neighborhood, don't worry, Jesus knows the way. If you run into some people you don't know, don't worry, Jesus knows what to say. If you see something you've never seen before, don't worry, Jesus can help you understand.

A Passionate Life

No doubt you can add to this list your own personal reasons for avoiding discipleship. But you're reading this book, so you're seeking discipleship, not avoiding it. That's the place to start.

LifeShapes is not an eight-step program to spiritual maturity. It's not a guaranteed-or-your-money-back scheme. It's simply a visual set of reminders of the things Jesus wants us to learn as we walk with him. Anyone can use this visual set of reminders. Just get out pencil and paper to get started.

Sketch a couple of shapes at the top of your planner each day so you'll seem them repeatedly and be reminded of what Jesus taught.

Draw shapes on sticky-notes and put them around the house.

Challenge yourself to see these shapes in the everyday items around you. The hole on a golf course. The roof that makes a triangle. Traffic signs. A tree that you realize has seven main branches. A note on a notepad. A toddler's toy. The pattern in the weave of your sweater.

Jesus calls us to passionate discipleship. You're passionate about something that you care about deeply, something that stirs deep emotions in you, something that you feel right to your core.

A passionate walk with Jesus.

A passionate faith that spills over into everything we do.

A passionate energy for the kingdom of God.

A passionate conviction to minister to those around you.

A passionate search for others ready to meet Jesus.

A passionate life.

The Word at Work Around the World

A vital part of Cook Communications Ministries is our international outreach, Cook Communications Ministries International (CCMI). Your purchase of this book, and of other books and Christian-growth products from Cook, enables CCMI to provide Bibles and Christian literature to people in more than 150 languages in 65 countries.

Cook Communications Ministries is a not-for-profit, self-supporting organization. Revenues from sales of our books, Bible curricula, and other church and home products not only fund our U.S. ministry, but also fund our CCMI ministry around the world. One hundred percent of donations to CCMI go to our international literature programs.

CCMI reaches out internationally in three ways:

• Our premier International Christian Publishing Institute (ICPI) trains leaders from nationally led publishing houses around the world.

• We provide literature for pastors, evangelists, and Christian workers in their national language.

• We reach people at risk—refugees, AIDS victims, street children, and famine victims—with God's Word.

Word Power, God's Power

Faith Kidz, RiverOak, Honor, Life Journey, Victor, NexGen — every time you purchase a book produced by Cook Communications Ministries, you not only meet a vital personal need in your life or in the life of someone you love, but you're also a part of ministering to José in Colombia, Humberto in Chile, Gousa in India, or Lidiane in Brazil. You help make it possible for a pastor in China, a child in Peru, or a mother in West Africa to enjoy a life-changing book. And because you helped, children and adults around the world are learning God's Word and walking in his ways.

Thank you for your partnership in helping to disciple the world. May God bless you with the power of his Word in your life.

For more information about our international ministries, visit www.ccmi.org.

LIFE SHAPES

Building a generation of *passionate* believers

Join the LifeShapes community –
Check us out online at: www.lifeshapes.com

- View sample chapters of future LifeShapes publications – before you can buy them in the stores!

- Post your thoughts/experiences on our bulletin board

- Connect with others whose lives are being changed through the LifeShapes movement!

- Download LifeShapes streaming audio & video features authors Michael Breen & Walt Kallestad

- Sign up for future online training events with LifeShapes trainers

- Feed your passion: Subscribe to the monthly LifeShapes e-newsletter

And much more!

We can't wait to see you online! Log on today!

LIFESHAPES.COM

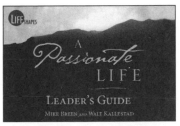
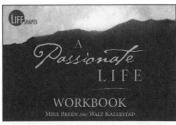